The Best of On My Mind

Ordering Information

Additional copies of *The Best of On My Mind: The Bryan Times Newspaper Columns of Don Allison,* may be purchased for $15.95, plus $4 shipping and handling, from Faded Banner Publications, P.O. Box 101, Bryan, OH 43506, telephone 1-888-799-3787 (toll free), or on the Web at www.fadedbanner.com. Dealer inquiries are welcome.

The Best of On My Mind

The Bryan Times Newspaper Columns of Don Allison

By Donald L. Allison

Faded Banner Publications

Bryan, Ohio

Library of Congress Catalogue Number: 2014919222

The Best of On My Mind: The Bryan Times Newspaper Columns of Don Allison

Donald L. Allison

Cover design by Stuart Rosebrock

ISBN   978-0-9659201- 4-8

First Printing

I dedicate this book to my parents

Acknowledgments

I wish to thank The Bryan Times for providing an outlet for my passion for journalism for more than three decades, and for the opportunity to write a weekly column. I've been granted nearly total freedom of expression on a weekly basis, and for that I am grateful.

I am forever indebted to my parents, Jimmie and Charles Allison, for their encouragement in pursuing an education and exploring what life has to offer, and for their total support in whatever I have attempted in life.

My wife, Diane, has been an invaluable source of inspiration and support. She has offered insightful critiques of my work, and had indulged my writing whims. Our sons, siblings and their families have been very understanding of my observations regarding our lives, and for that I am grateful.

I am extremely grateful for the readers of my columns, who countless times have commented on columns they especially enjoyed. Even when someone has disliked what I have written, I value the input and appreciate the fact that they care. I am especially humbled when readers take the time to call, email or drop me a note to share how a column has touched their lives. It is such moments that enrich my life as a writer.

Table of Contents

The space is empty, so I'll try to make it home

This column appeared on September 29. 2006. Although Don had written columns for years, and had earned Associated Press awards for his efforts, the columns had not appeared on a regular basis. With the retirement of Times Senior Editor Linda Freed, who had written a weekly column, Don stepped in as her replacement. This was his initial regular column, and his first under the new On My Mind *title.*

I feel like someone who has just acquired a bigger, fancier house. Right now I'm walking around the empty rooms, trying to imagine how I'm going to decorate and furnish it, how to make it home.

The house was big and beautiful under the watch of the former owner. I'm used to seeing it as the previous occupant kept it for many years — well decorated, comfortable, home.

Now those rooms seem so big and bare, begging to be brought back to life.

During the retirement dinner for Times Senior Editor Linda Freed someone asked if I planned to write a column.

When I replied yes, although I couldn't promise it will be weekly, someone asked if I would be writing about Lyle. If I do, I responded, joining in the laughter, I'll have to undertake some research.

As I'm sure nearly all Bryan Times readers are aware, Lyle is Linda's husband. Linda's life with Lyle was a frequent part of her column *Editor's Notebook* that appeared each Friday in the Times. Through the years Linda wrote more than 2,000 columns, initially under the title *Thoughts from Under the Dryer*.

Because of those columns, the Freeds are probably the best known family in Williams County.

Linda's retirement leaves a hole in our Friday Page of Opinion *where Editor's Notebook* used to appear. It also leaves a yearning from her legions of fans.

There's no way I could duplicate Linda's column. I would never even try. All I can do is wander around this empty Friday editorial page space, trying to figure out how to make it home.

I've written a few *Second Thoughts* columns through the years. Through them I've tried to be funny or entertaining, pay tribute to friends and family, and address some serious issues facing the community.

Second Thoughts is a staff-generated column, open to Times writers. *Editor's Notebook* is decidedly Linda's column.

For several weeks I've kicked about possible names for a column of my own. After deliberating over scores of titles, some possibly good and some probably not so good, I've settled on one.

I'll call it *On My Mind*.

For this first column, what's on my mind is most definitely the legacy Linda Freed left behind at the Times. Beyond her columns, Linda was a steadying, influential force for myself and many, many other employees during her 40 years at the newspaper.

I'm thankful for the chance to know Linda for almost my entire life – long, long before I joined the Times staff – and for the chance to work with and learn from her at the Times for more than a quarter century.

In future weeks, and hopefully months and years to come, I'll share what I have to offer in this Friday space. Maybe not every week, but I'll try to write frequently.

Perhaps for now I could do a bit of research about Lyle. Actually, that could be a bit interesting. My Dad and Lyle were high school classmates, and I bet there are a few stories there to be told ...

Anyway, Lyle stories or not, check back later. I'll try to make my column worth your while.

———

Clouds looming over dream home sunset

This column appeared on November 3, 2006, and addresses the battle earlier that year over plans to construct an egg-laying facility not far from Don's home – a plan that carried serious consequences for the quality of life for those living in the vicinity of that egg farm.

L avenders, pinks and highlights of gold spread across the scattered clouds, a glowing farewell from the evening sun dipping behind the distant trees.

I laid my bricks aside, transfixed at the scene. The wind rustled gently through the brown stalks of corn, a bird walked leisurely across the top of the zigzag rail fence. Slowly, deeply I breathed in, savoring the fall scent of walnut husks and falling leaves.

And slowly I exhaled, finding it almost impossible to believe I wasn't dreaming, but standing in the yard of what I will soon call home.

The old brick house Diane and I are restoring is truly the country home of our dreams. With its original woodwork, windows and floors, it literally drips with the history of Williams County's earliest settlers.

Those giant maple and walnut trees, the lush grass of the yard, the woods that line the creek behind the fields of corn and wheat, all greeted the eyes of generations of farmers who have called the old house home.

The grass still grows thickest in the old barnyard, which countless cattle, horses, sheep, chickens and other livestock naturally fertilized through the years. Livestock is long gone now, but the old barn still reigns. Not a part of our homestead purchase, the grand old structure still houses farm machinery and straw, still an integral part of a farm that's remained in the same family for 137 years.

I can't possibly imagine a more classical rural scene – a more traditional agricultural setting.

When I think our country dream may be destroyed, I feel a sickening, deadening weight in the pit of my stomach.

And how ironic that the agent of that destruction is a proposed factory billing itself as agriculture.

An egg-laying facility to house millions of chickens has been proposed for Williams County. One rumored location is not far from our dream home, upwind at that. Last spring I viewed a similar facility outside of Malcom, Iowa. I talked to the egg facility's operators, and to people who live in and around Malcom and the chicken barns.

Nearly every local resident mentioned one thing about the chicken facility.

The smell.

A smell that some say keeps them virtual prisoners in their own homes at times, unable to even open their windows for fresh air. Showing in the residents' eyes and revealed in their voices as they talk about the smell is the emotion, a mixture of resignation and despair.

Living in the country has been our dream for years. Diane spent much of her youth living on farms. Even as a "city boy" growing up in Stryker the crops grew only yards away and I made spending money working on farms — baling hay, hoeing and cutting weeds, repairing old clay farm tiles.

Anyone who has lived for long in northwest Ohio knows that dust, noise and the smell of manure are a part of country living. What they also know is the smell is manageable, unpleasantly strong only a few days a year.

But factory farms can have thousands of times more animals than our traditional farms, and can impact neighbors' quality of life accordingly. In my mind, these behemoths bear no more resemblance to traditional farms than a giant car production facility does to a family horse-drawn carriage shop.

As battle lines form between the factory farms and the neighbors being robbed of enjoying the outdoors, state officials have tilted the table towards the megafarmers. State legislators have taken away local control and regulation of such farms — if the operations meet state standards, as regulated by the Ohio Department of Agriculture, there's nothing local folks can do about it.

Smell, by the way, is not regulated.

For two years Diane and I have poured our hearts and souls into our country acre, the place we plan to call home for the rest of our lives. I'm not willing to sacrifice sitting on the porch or working in the yard so some out-of-area or even out-of-state investors can increase their profits.

That's especially true for investors who don't build the chicken coops or cow barns behind their own homes, like on a traditional family farm, but instead locate them behind somebody else's house, to let someone else bear the cost associated with the profit.

Even if the chicken factory doesn't locate near my dream country home or yours, the way the rules are drawn now, some other factory farm likely will.

If you live in a rural agricultural area of Ohio, your quality of life is at risk. The only thing you can do about that is to get the attention of your state senators and representatives — be it through the ballot box, letters, phone calls, public meetings, or whatever else you can think of.

Love family farmers, support family farmers, leave family farmers be. But when it comes to megafarms, limit them and regulate them like the factories that they are.

Should enough people show they care, perhaps our future vistas will continue to be farm fields, sunsets and trees, and our scents those of flowers, falling leaves and walnut husks.

————

It's got to be a breeze, from do-it-yourself TV

This column appeared January 12, 2007, and is based on experiences renovating our 1835 farmhouse.

I must confess, my wife and I are HGTV, DIY and This Old House junkies.

After watching a few episodes of the do-it-yourself shows, we're ready to reroof the house, build a custom garage, add on a family room, and create a landscaped garden complete with 20-foot stone fountain — all in one weekend, with time to relax Sunday evening to boot.

You've all seen the shows, the ones that demonstrate just how easy it is to demolish that decades-old bathroom and create the washroom of your dreams.

When you actually do it yourself, it takes only that first 70-year-old rusted cast iron toilet drain to tax your mixed-company vocabulary.

By the time you've iced down those throbbing knuckles after the pipe wrench slipped off that final time, you're ready to conclude the washroom of your dreams may well include a pre World War II commode.

And the following weekend, when you tackle that old bathtub, it's suddenly become the washroom of your worst nightmares.

I feel like I ought to pitch my own do-it-yourself show, based on actual projects I've undertaken — true reality TV.

My most recent project, replacement of a basement door at our historic brick house, could be the pilot episode.

Removing the old deteriorated door should be a breeze, I would tell the audience in opening the show. Just take a chisel and heavy hammer, and knock the hinge pins out.

My ineffective hammer swings, of course interspersed with bleeped-out comments, would take us to the first commercial break — and well beyond, if not for merciful editing.

After returning from the commercial, I would confess just how difficult 160-year-old exterior door hinge pins are to remove, and note that removing the hinges from the door frame — with the door still attached — would be a viable alternative.

Experienced do-it-yourselfers in the audience could share my pain as I scrape countless coats of paint from the slots of the old screws, then proceed to demonstrate how well those screws still hold in the old hardwood frame.

Eleven of the 12 screws holding the three hinges, the audience would learn, could not be budged.

But I would hold the one bent, stripped-but-now-removed-screw triumphantly, leading to the next commercial break.

A return from commercial would show me at the old door, placing the proper sized bit into a drill so I could simply drill out the old screws.

After I realized the batteries in the drill were nearly drained, the audience could watch and listen as I ransacked the house for the plug-in drill.

Next week, they would learn, I could actually try drilling out those screws.

Should the networks take the bait, in episodes to follow I would actually be seen drilling out the old screws, falling to the floor as the heavy old door finally lurched free of its moorings.

Audiences would meet the Ace Hardware staff when I traveled to town after realizing I'd lost the drill bit of the size I needed to install the replacement door and hinges.

Soon, audiences would meet the Town and Country Hardware staff, where I went to get the screws I'd forgotten at Ace, and not wanting the Ace staff to think I was an idiot running back five minutes later for something else.

In weeks to come, the audience would come to know the Town and Country and Ace staffs as familiar old friends.

Audiences also would learn to appreciate the cardiovascular workout that comes from running up and down the stairs repeatedly in quest of lost or forgotten tools.

They would learn countless ways not to anchor an out-of-square hardwood frame to the old bricks backing it, and several techniques that don't work when mortising out an antique oak door to install a lock.

And much, much, much more, if the networks would have the foresight to go ahead with my show.

Just think, season two could feature refurbishing those 160-year-old window frames.

If they only gave Emmys for creative language, by that point I'd be polishing my acceptance speech.

———

A blast from the past
brings benefits today

This column appeared on January 24, 2007.

I t is indeed a blast from the past.

Twenty-nine years ago an epic arctic front slashed across northwest Ohio, leaving behind snowdrifts as high as houses. The area was paralyzed for days. Power lines snapped by near hurricane-force winds left many residents shivering without heat in the bitter cold.

For those who experienced it, the Blizzard of '78 is unforgettable.

The storm was still fresh on the minds of WBNO radio staff a year later, when they decided to commemorate the blizzard with an event to benefit the community. Thus the Blizzard Auction was born.

Each year, on the Saturday closest to the Blizzard of '78 anniversary, the station conducts a radio auction to benefit a local organization. Usually tens of thousands of dollars are generated. Local businesses, organizations and individuals donate the items that are sold to raise the cash.

Although I've often bid on and purchased Blizzard Auction items, this Saturday will be the first time I've actually helped out with the event. I'm a trustee of the Williams County Historical Society, this year's beneficiary, so my wife and I will help manage the flow of auctioned items.

I'm excited the Historical Society will get this much-needed boost. The list of necessary repairs to conserve the society's historic sites alone — not including any operational needs — exceeds $100,000. So pardon me if I urge you to bid high, and bid often.

The Blizzard of '78 is truly a part of history now. It is hard for me to comprehend that anyone younger than 35 or so would have no recollections of the storm. As such, it is only appropriate that the Historical Society benefits from the Blizzard Auction.

Even though I wasn't in Williams County during the Blizzard of '78 — I was a student at the University of Toledo, living near campus — I have my own personal history of the Great Storm.

On Jan. 25 heavy rains fell, and I remember being soaked running out to grab a late snack. We watched the 11 p.m. news, and scoffed at the newscasters predicting massive amounts of snow and bitter, cold winds that would whip up drifts of 15 meet or more.

The next morning I awoke to my roommate's radio, with the DJ talking about cancellations. He said the list was simple — everything was closed.

We found his description of the city hard to believe. When we looked out the bedroom window overlooking the apartment complex parking lot, all we saw was white. No cars, no people, no pathways — just white, with barely perceptible lumps showing where some of the cars were buried. And the snow was still falling.

The fact that we were low on food should have bothered us, but being college students we had bigger worries.

We had no beer.

So off we went on foot, braving the snow and arctic winds.

Our first stop was a grocery store near campus, but the manager locked the doors in our faces. He refused to let us in, despite our pleas, yelling through the glass that he was closing due to the emergency.

The next nearest store was way across campus, a daunting trek considering many of the snow drifts towered over our heads. We seemed to have found an easy way across one parking lot, walking atop a frozen wall of snow remaining from previous plowings.

It was a good way to go until my roommate — an offensive lineman on the UT football team who was more than six feet tall — simply disappeared into the snow ahead of me. We had come to the end of the frozen snow wall, and fortunately my roommate suffered only a slightly twisted ankle in the fall.

Our luck held out when the next store was open, and well stocked.

Arms full of supplies, we struggled back to the apartment, which fortunately still had power. Many fellow students on campus and to the north of us went without electricity for days.

While holed up in the apartment I got a call from my grandmother in Alabama. She had seen Toledo on the news, and wanted to be sure I was OK. She had just watched U.S. Army Reserves digging out a Toledo railroad underpass that was completely blocked with snow.

I told her we were fine — I didn't want to worry her by noting the underpass she saw on TV was visible from my bedroom window.

The first few days were just a vacation. Later, as the city dug out, we helped each other excavate the snowbanks in search of our vehicles.

For weeks no pavement was visible on any of the city's streets, even the main ones, as about eight inches of ice and compacted snow provided the driving surface. When it began to melt, walking anywhere near a roadway was courting a cold-water shower from passing cars.

A VW Beetle owned by a friend was buried probably 25 feet inside a snow pile. He didn't even try to dig it out. The car stayed inside the snowbank until it melted away in March.

Even then he didn't drive it, or even try to start it.

He sold it instead.

Today that same VW would be included in classic car show. And the eight-track tapes we listened to while the blizzard winds howled outside, the Pong video game we played, are now appropriate for a museum.

Perhaps they could find a home in the Williams County Historical Society museum, where someday a display of the Blizzard of '78 might capture the imaginations of future young visitors.

———

We're not all-knowing, but we'd sure like to be

This column appeared on February 7, 2007.

I n an ideal world, a basic requirement for a journalist —
especially a newspaper editor — would be omniscience.

In effect, that means being all-knowing.

Unfortunately, only God meets that requirement.

So the journalistic jobs fall to us mere mortals.

Perhaps the most frustrating part of my decades of work at
the Times has been dealing with people who can't
understand why the Times didn't run a particular story.
They know about it, so why don't the people at the paper?

As I said, omniscience would be great.

But us not knowing shouldn't be confused with us not
wanting to know, or not caring. We go to great lengths to
see that stories don't pass us by. Each day we have staff
members poring over police and fire logs, and court filings,
so it if is a public record, we are aware of it.

We keep track of the meeting times and places of local
school boards, councils, commissions and similar bodies,
so our staff and the public can attend meetings. When we

cannot attend a session, we call to find out what transpired, and share it with our readers. We keep track of "sunshine laws" for open records and open meetings, so we are aware of the public records to which we are entitled. Information on these laws are shared with local public officials annually, and anytime a potential secrecy issue arises.

And we keeps our eyes and ears open to what people in the community are doing and saying.

Of course, that doesn't mean things won't get by us. Officials can skirt the sunshine law provisions, or take advantage of gray areas. Human beings can make inadvertent mistakes, such as a public official not filing something they should, or a journalist overlooking something they should seize on.

Sometimes, the best stories come to us through tips from our readers. These often are things outside the official public record, but can make the best stories of all.

Once a reader told me about a woman who raised a litter of orphaned baby flying squirrels, that were accidentally brought into her house in the hollowed out portion of a firewood log. The woman faithfully nursed them every few hours, even in the middle of the night.

Interviewing her as the baby squirrels ran and glided through her kitchen was an fascinating experience. It's one I'll never forget, and one that Times readers mentioned to me for months after.

A more recent story involved a Times rural carrier who went into labor while delivering the paper — when she delivers, she really delivers, the headline stated. It was a great human interest story, shared to us by a family member of the carrier.

Even more recently, we learned of a dog rescued from the Lake Seneca ice by a compassionate neighbor. Again, a news tip made the difference — as it has countless times in my career.

And we appreciate those tips. If you know of a potentially interesting story, give our editorial department a call at 419-636-1111 and share it with us. It may just be the type of story we're looking for.

Of course, not every news tip pans out. Sometimes people involved in a great story decide they don't want to share it with us publicly. Maybe we've already run the story earlier.

Sometimes the story involves alleged wrongdoing, when no former charges or allegations have been made. In other cases incidents involve personal disputes, such as between an individual and a business or divorcing spouses over child custody, that we feel have no place in the Times pages.

Other times, a tip might lead to a memorable story of the year — or, at the very least, a listing of honors earned by a friend or relative here or with ties to northwest Ohio.

So please keep us in mind.

———

It's a tough call; who holds referee whistle?

This column appeared on February 16, 2007.

Sometimes, even the planks of the fence have splinters.

It can be tough to remain objective when a controversial topic grips a town, such as Rite Aid's planned relocation in Bryan.

As a newspaper The Times tries to remain above the fray, and accurately present the pros and cons raised in debate. While the storm rages, we believe our best course is to navigate — and illuminate — the flow of ideas.

In the case of Rite Aid's plan, two elements very important to the community come into play.

On the one hand, a business is looking not only to maintain its presence in the community, but to expand. Rite Aid is looking to build a bigger, modern, more centrally located facility. The new pharmacy will provide jobs and enhance the community's tax base.

In today's economy of northwest Ohio, those are important considerations.

On the other hand, the new facility will encroach on the city's historic district. Many Bryan property owners have invested considerable time and money — in some cases, parts of their heart and soul — into restoring and preserving parts of the city's past, its heritage.

Once gone, a historic home never can be replaced. Where one person sees a rundown, ramshackle eyesore, another may see a potential historic jewel.

When existing older structures are involved, development is always a balancing act of sorts.

Is it fair to tell a business — a firm seeking to keep pace in an increasingly competitive market — that it cannot locate where it wants to locate, on a main thoroughfare across from a rival?

Or, is it fair to tell a property owner who has purchased a home in a historic district, expecting the neighborhood to remain historic and residential, that the view out their front door will soon be the rear side and lighted parking lot area of a modern store?

Some people have urged me personally, and others at The Times, to take a stand. I'll have to admit this is an especially difficult issue for me. I am a firm believer in the importance of saving our history, preserving key parts of our past. I am even now in the process of restoring one of Williams County's oldest homes myself, although it is just outside of Bryan.

But let me stress that I also see economic development and vitality, a tax base and jobs, as absolutely necessary to our community's future.

That, folks, makes it a tough call.

I don't believe it is the role of The Bryan Times staff to decide the issue. That is up to the members of city council. What the role of The Times should be is to keep the public informed, to present the facts of the case and foster informed debate.

Latest developments show the give and take of democracy may be working in this case. In discussion at Monday's Planning and Zoning Commission meeting, Rite Aid officials appeared willing to adapt the facility's design to help blend in with the historic district. We can see how this goes.

In a democracy we must trust our elected leaders to sort out the pros and cons — preferably guided by citizens putting forth their best ideas, accurate unbiased news reporting, and their own personal research — and reach the best decision.

If we don't agree with that conclusion, we do have some recourse. There's always the next election.

———

Winter winds whip up
old faded news footage

This column appeared on February 23, 2007.

The reality struck with the force of the wintry winds. Great events of my adulthood have been reduced to old dated, faded news footage.

A week ago Tuesday I sat in my recliner in front of the TV, still panting from my battle with the snowblower and the frigid gusts. I watched the meteorologists and parka-clad reporters dissect the developing winter blast. The events of course sparked comparisons with the great Blizzard of '78, the standard by which all modern snowstorms are judged.

I don't use the term "great" lightly in this case. At the time I didn't fully appreciate the magnitude of the 1978 storm, the force that Mother Nature unleashed on northwest Ohio. My memories of the 1978 blizzard are vivid. I can still feel the sting of the cold wind and driving snow as my college friends and I trekked in search of life-sustaining food and beverages. We were young and robust and making the best of one of life's great adventures.

While comparing the relatively paltry Blizzard of '07 to the '78 blast, the newscast I was watching cut to archival footage from January 1978. I recoiled at the faded colors, the outlandish clothing and haircuts, the crudeness of the videotape. It came across as ancient history, the distant past resurrected for today's young people to digest.

As I watched I felt the muscles of my lower back slowly stiffen, the price I was paying for a temporarily passable driveway. At least those tired, tightening muscles could keep my heart from sinking too far. While I've been busy living, geezerhood has snuck up on me.

At different times in life, events or perceptions drive home the reality of time's relentless pace. You don't feel older, you don't think older, you don't act older. And you don't think you look so much older, until one day you see that older person looking back at you from the mirror.

All my life I've been fascinated by the old scratchy, grainy black-and-white news footage of events beyond my own memory, or from my distant childhood. But they depict old happenings, not events from my own adulthood. Perhaps I should take solace from my advancing age. Perhaps people will look to me, hoping I'll share the wisdom and knowledge of my experience. Maybe my grandson will buy that, but I can already hear my wife and sons laughing at the idea, so maybe I'll just keep this one to myself.

At any rate I'll adjust, just like I've adjusted to bifocal lenses, an expanding middle, a low-fat diet and ridiculous fashion changes. As an older friend of mine likes to say, at least I'm on the right side of the grass.

Or in this case, the snow.

What's on my mind?
I want to say thanks

This column appeared March 2, 2007.

I t's hard to believe I'm in my sixth month of sharing what's "On My Mind."

So far I've been seldom cussed, and often complimented. For that I'm grateful, and humbled as well.

I had no idea how my new column would be received. I've had some giant footsteps to fill, a Times Page of Opinion vacancy left by the retirement of long-time Times columnist Linda Freed. Linda had built a considerable, loyal readership in her career, and I had no idea how this upstart replacement would fare.

Could I come up with something interesting – once a week, no less — that would be worth readers' time to digest?

Would anyone care about my childhood memories of Bryan's Christmas lights? Are my thoughts on my parents' 50th wedding anniversary enough to hold readers' interest? Really, did anyone care about my spaghetti dinner when a Detroit Tigers' home run took them to the

World Series, or the role being a Tiger fan has played in my life?

And, seriously, would anyone find my experiences replacing an old door to be entertaining?

It began slowly at first, people stopping me on the street or making a phone call to the Times, telling me how much they enjoyed this or that column. As I've continued to write, those comments, calls and e-mails have become more and more frequent.

Almost uniformly those comments have been positive, and encouraging. Even when a reader is calling me to task about something, I've found it valuable — it lets me know you're reading what I have to write.

I've truly appreciated the chance to share my opinions on important issues facing the community. Not everyone has agreed with everything I've had to write on these topics, but I've been able to throw my thoughts as a newspaper editor into the mix. It's a privilege — no, really more a responsibility — that I do not take lightly.

Even before committing to be a weekly columnist, writing a column was certainly not foreign to me. Among my proudest career accomplishments are Associated Press Society of Ohio awards I've received for my earlier Second Thoughts columns.

The difference is that my Second Thoughts installments were sporadic, not regular. I could write them only when the inspiration struck, and lay off a month or two — or even three — if sufficient stimulation should be lacking.

And that's really the rub of a regular column. Some columns come to me as if by magic. They fly from my mind to the keyboard, my fingers barely able to keep up with my thoughts. Other times the computer screen — and my mind — are as vacant and featureless as a snow-covered farm field on a dreary February day.

But through thick and thin, readers have stayed with me, and encouraged me. For that, I offer my sincere thanks.

And for better or for worse, I'll keep sharing what's on my mind.

———

For citizens' sake, let the light shine in

This column appeared on March 9, 2007. Don addresses Sunshine Week, which highlights the value of open meeting and open records laws and the need for transparency in government.

If it involves public money, public employees or public facilities, it should be crystal clear. It's the public's business.

So let the light shine in.

That's the basis of the Ohio Sunshine Law and Federal Freedom of Information Act – and by the way, the foundation of democracy itself. There's even a designated Sunshine Week, March 11 to 17, to highlight openness in government. Initiated by Florida newspapers, Sunshine Week is now a national event headed by the American Society of Newspaper Editors in conjunction with the Coalition of Journalists for Open Government.

In a nutshell, "Sunshine" laws reflect a belief that in a democracy the public has a right to know what its government is doing. Some with a cynical bent might put it differently, who is doing what to whom. But like anything, it really isn't that simple.

As long as the United States and Ohio have existed, government officials have tried to keep a cloak over some proceedings. And various crusaders in the public and media — and on occasion government officials, agencies and courts — have done battle to keep information public.

Since Sept. 11 the war on terror has thrown an unparalleled blanket of secrecy on many government functions — even some court proceedings — that could be perceived as a threat to Americans' basic individual rights and freedom.

In Ohio, the open vs. secret battle was played out recently in the State Senate and House of Representatives. The result was an amended version of Ohio's Sunshine Law, which outlines which organizations are public bodies required to conduct open meetings, and which records are indeed available to citizens.

Of course, there are instances when records or meetings should be closed to the public, at least temporarily. One example is complaints against a public official, in which those charges are not yet verified. It would be unfair to air unsubstantiated allegations against someone who may well be innocent, and sully his or her good name in the public eye. The same goes for criminal investigations.

Other understandable exceptions include security arrangements of public agencies, and some personal information about law enforcement officers.

At the state level the result of those conflicting interests is a complicated law, full of definitions of what constitutes public bodies and public records, and lists and lists of exemptions to openness. This law is certainly confusing for most citizens, and can vex even a well-intentioned government employee or official.

In that light, one favorable provision of the revised Ohio legislation is a requirement for all elected government officials to attend training and seminars on the Ohio public records law. The Ohio attorney general is charged with developing that training. The attorney general also is charged with developing a model public records policy, to guide officials in developing their own office's policies. And the auditor of state is required to audit public offices for compliance.

These provisions of the new law are effective Sept. 29 of this year.

When it comes to open records and open meetings, I believe the laws and courts should err on the side of openness, for the sake of having an informed citizen base.

Unfortunately, in my years of newspaper work, I've seen some officials who try to keep information out of the public's hands — information that unquestionably belongs in the public sphere.

The easier it is to keep things secret, the more things will be kept secret — even information that has no business being hidden. Sometimes keeping a lid something makes an official's job easier, free of public complaints or meddling. Or, sometimes information can be embarrassing.

I don't mean to paint all officials with a sweeping, critical brush, because many, many officials I've dealt with have been nothing but open, helpful and above board. But you don't have to look too far to see what secrecy can do. Just consider Coingate — Ohio's rare coin investment scandal and associated Bureau of Workers Compensation investment problems.

When open meetings and records provisions are threatened, newspapers and other media are quick to cry foul. Those protests are meaningful, and often effective.

But in the end our access to information about what our government is up to rests upon our own efforts, our own awareness as citizens. People must show interest in the government, and demand an open, transparent operation.

Without that, the cloak of darkness may well obscure the sun.

———

That daylight savings comes at a high cost

This column appeared on March 15, 2007.

Beep by piercing beep by piercing beep the alarm chiseled its way into my unconsciousness.

Pokes and moans from my half-asleep wife shoved me unwillingly into a dim state of awareness, that the rhythmic shriek was my wake-up call. It was Monday, time to get up, time to start the day.

And time to turn off the alarm, except that my arm was pinned under my pillow. It was fast asleep in its own right, paralyzed and powerless.

Still came the clock's pulsating screeches, and Diane's pokes of frustration, as I swung my functionless arm time and again at the clock. Finally, after a tortuous eternity, I activated the snooze alarm.

And I went right back to sleep, only to be reawakened when the alarm blared again in what seemed to be milliseconds later.

Welcome to Daylight Savings Time.

If you're like me – far from a morning person – 5 a.m. comes awfully early anytime. When your biological clock is stuck on Eastern Standard Time, being forced out of bed an hour early is a torture straight out of the Spanish Inquisition.

It may be Daylight Savings, but I definitely pay a price for the switch.

Granted, that extra hour of evening light is nice, especially for someone like me who enjoys being outdoors. But March weather often keeps us stuck inside anyway, and April seems plenty early to me for making the time switch.

For days to come I'll continue to suffer from time lag. I feel a bit dazed, a bit confused, out of step.

Tuesday it seemed the time change had thrown my whole world out of kilter. After my second straight day of not quite being with it at work, having trouble with such basic tasks as deciphering a calendar, I concluded the warm sunshine offered the perfect opportunity to change the thermostat in my old truck.

I estimated the job at 15 minutes, had it all but done in 12, but as I was refilling the radiator with antifreeze I saw a green stream begin to flow from the bottom of the thermostat housing. Close inspection revealed a crack

It turns out I hadn't properly seated the new thermostat, putting stress on the housing. Forty-five minutes later, after a trip to the store to acquire a replacement housing, I was bolting the new housing in place when a crack appeared on this part — same place, same cause. Another trip to a parts store found them out of stock on the housing, but able to order a new one in a day.

With that project on hold, my son Joe joined me for a trip to the old house Diane and I am restoring. A noise upstairs alerted me that a bird had found its way inside. Fortunately I was able to safely corral the bird with a painting tarp, setting it free outside.

So far at the house, so good.

Until I decided to open up the windows to allow the warm fresh air inside. On the first window I tackled the new storm window, instead of sliding smoothly open, came loose in my hand. Five minutes later, after fighting with the tabs that hold it in place, I turned it over to Joe.

He quickly slid the window in place, but as soon as he did the halogen work light in the room began to flicker, as the bulb died in flashings of slowly fading yellow light. Left in the gathering Daylight Savings Time dusk, I decided to call it a day.

At fake bedtime that night, I lay there wide awake — an hour before true bedtime, of course — looking ahead to that jolting 5 a.m. — no fooling my body, 4 a.m. — wakeup call.

————

As if by magic, today's news hits your door

This column appeared on March 30, 2007.

Your screen door creaks open, you hear the thump of the paper, and there it is, today's news. Ready to read, digest, and enjoy — or complain about, if the mood strikes you.

Every day but Sunday, six days a week, The Bryan Times is there.

It must be magic, right?

As much as it would make our job at the Times easier, it isn't magic. As with many things, the hard work is behind the scenes. It's like a rock group's road crew spending hours building the stage, rolling in the amps, setting up the lights, and wiring up the sound before the big concert.

Then — just like the road crew — we do it all over again tomorrow.

It can seem so easy. You read the story on the accident you heard about at the store. There's the piece on the city council's controversial zoning change your neighbor complained about. On Today's Log you see the list of arrests — maybe your co-worker's cousin is in trouble again.

Gathering news must be just like plucking apples from a tree, right? Isn't it just there for the taking? That is somewhat correct, such as for our international, national and state news over the Associated Press wire. We receive hundreds of wire stories and photos each day that we sort through, picking and choosing what we think are the best of AP's offerings.

But local news — our bread and butter, what most people really look to the Times to provide — is often an entirely different story. It would be nice if we could be omniscient and omnipresent — all-knowing and all present, a bit like God, if you will. But, of course, we're not.

You may not think twice about how that car accident photo came to be on Page 1. For a minute, though, please do consider it. How did we know the accident happened — and in that small window of time, get a photographer there on the scene? And how did we know the details — who was ticketed, who was hurt, who was taken to which hospital, and the conditions of the injured people?

As much as we can, we're constantly monitoring what's going on. In the newsroom we have a television tuned to a news channel, and a scanner set to local emergency frequencies. Our photographers even have an emergency scanner to use at their homes. If we hear of a fire, accident or other emergency we can immediately send staff members or photographers to the scene.

Once we've got that accident photo, then comes the newsgathering. Which police agency investigated? We find out and phone them to ask what caused the accident, and whether anyone was cited. Was anyone hurt? We find out from the police agency who was injured and where they were taken for treatment, and phone each hospital for the injured people's conditions. Was someone transferred to a different hospital? There's another phone call. Someone's name is spelled two different ways? More checking, to find out which version is correct.

Were fire departments called? That may necessitate another phone call for details of their involvement.

And a question we dread, was anyone killed? If so, we find out which funeral home is handling arrangements, and contact the mortuary for details.

If the accident happens early in the morning, we're doing all this under the pressure of a looming deadline, to get it in today's paper.

And any story, any time, can require this much work or more.

News is a 24/7 job. Times staff members read other papers, listen to radio news, watch TV, and keep an ear tuned for news tips from neighbors and friends. That controversial council meeting you read about? That story didn't just pop out of nowhere into the news pages. A Times staffer sat through that two-hour evening meeting — after a full day in the office of course — and likely spent another hour or two writing the story after the meeting was over.

If questions remained in the writer's mind after the meeting, he or she may have spend a while at the town hall asking questions, or making follow-up phone calls at the office.

Those local sports stories and photos? Our sports staff keeps track of the schedule of local events, and our writers and reporters drive to the games, gather the pertinent information, and are back at the office that night, writing the stories and preparing the photos for publication.

Are there more games than we could possible send staff members to? Then there are reporters manning the phones, getting the pertinent information from the involved coaches.

Each day someone from the Times visits or calls the local police agencies, and checks in at the 9-1-1 central dispatch, and the courts.

Other Times staffers sort through mails and emails, check out news tips and handle phone calls each day, finding out who's engaged, who's been married, who's on the dean's list, who's gotten a new job or a promotion, who died, and all the other important happenings in the lives of those in the local community. All this, of course, is done while facing deadlines of some sort or anther.

Thinking about it, maybe there's a bit of magic involved after all.

———

Observations ring true, even after 117 years

This column appeared on April 6, 2007.

How to Kill Your Town

That attention-catching phrase headlined an article that Carolyn Pfiester of Bryan discovered, a piece published in the March 21, 1890, edition of the Blissfield, Mich., Alliance newspaper. The article interested her, she explained, so she shared a copy with The Times.

Dating back 117 years, some of the references are of course dated. But with some modern adaptation, the observations ring as true today as they did in 1890.

So, just how do you kill your town?

"Buy of peddlers often and as much as possible," the article states. Of course, door-to-door salesmen aren't so prominent today, but just substitute online shopping and — point well taken.

The article continues:

"Denounce your merchants because they make profit on their goods.

"Glory in the downfall of a man who has done much to build up the town.

"Make your town out a very bad place and stab it every chance you get.

"Refuse to unite in any scheme for the betterment of the material interests of the people.

"Tell your merchant that you can buy goods a good deal cheaper in some other town and charge them with extortion.

"If a stranger comes to your town tell him everything is overdone, and predict a general crash in the town in the near future.

"Keep up divided public sentiment and knife every man that disagrees with you on the best method of increasing business.

"When you have anything to say about the town, say it in such a way that it will leave the impression that you have no faith in it.

"Patronize outside newspapers to the exclusion of your own, and then denounce yours for not being as large and cheap as the big city papers.

"If you are a merchant, don't advertise in the home paper, but buy a rubber stamp and use it. It may save you a few dimes and make the paper look as though it was published in a one horse town."

Rubber stamps might not be in vogue anymore, but a computer-generated brochure or flyer would certainly be today's equivalent.

"If you are a farmer," the article concludes, "curse the place where you trade as the meanest on earth. Talk this to your neighbors and tell them the business men are robbers and thieves. If till make your property much less valuable, but then you don't care."

———————

When letter arrives, it's a good day

This column appeared April 13, 2007.

I t was a good day when a letter from Grandma arrived.

I'd drop what I was doing, carefully rip open the envelop, then immerse myself in what Grandma had to say. I'd read it, read it again, put it away, then go back to it later. Before long I'd bring out a pen and paper and draft my reply.

From the time I first could read — and scratch out a crude return note of my own — exchanging letters with Grandma had been a treasured part of my life. We were 800 miles apart, typically seeing each other only for an all-too-brief time each summer, but the written word kept us together.

There was no earth-shattering news in Grandma's letters. Usually she wrote about who she'd visited with, what she'd been doing, how her flowers and garden were growing, what was up in the lives of my aunts, uncles and cousins. She'd also offer me valued advice.

And always was the finishing message, "Love, Grandma."

As I became a young adult, finishing my college education, the letters grew shorter, came less often. Those loving, labored lines became more and more difficult to decipher.

Her will to write was as strong as ever, but the arthritis in her fingers was creating a true writer's block.

In what I remember as her shortest letter, she confessed it would be the last as well. Her fingers were too stiff to write anymore, she noted, and we would have to settle for phone calls instead.

Not that I didn't treasure those telephone conversations. They continued for years, until just a few days before she died. Indeed, her last words to me, "I love you, babe," still ring in my ears.

But you can't hold a phone call, pull it out later, read every word again and again and again even many years later.

Sparking my recollection of Grandma's letters was a recent column by Times coworker Jay Ford Cullis. He observed how the written word brings two people together, overcoming the time difference between the writing and the reading.

When it comes right down to it the written word spans eternity — at least the portion of it occupied by the human race.

A couple of years ago a good friend gave me a book he thought I would enjoy, "Life in the Open Air." The author, Theodore Winthrop, was an up and coming young writer. In 1861, when the Civil War opened, he joined the Union army. Winthrop's life ended that year. He was one of the very first casualties of the war, killed in the June 10, 1861 Battle of Big Bethel, Va. His personal observations of the war, and other of his previously unpublished works, were compiled posthumously in 1863 in "Life in the Open Air."

A couple of months after I received the book I found the time to read it. At that point I had just returned from a vacation with my wife, Diane, to the north woods of Maine.

One of Winthrop's essays recounted how he followed nearly the identical route that Diane and I covered, across New Hampshire and into Maine, and on to Moosehead Lake. Travel was rougher in his day, typically on foot or by canoe, but his written portraits of the breathtaking wilderness painted exactly the same scenes Diane and I had just experienced.

A woodcut in the book even duplicated a photo Diane snapped on our own trip — the same lake, the same mountains in the background, the same angle from the shore.

By the time I sat "Life in the Open Air" down I felt like I had made a new friend, one who died nearly 145 years before. On more than one occasion, after a particularly stressful day, I've picked up Winthrop's book and reread some of his Maine travel passages, reliving a highlight of my own life.

Something I haven't picked up lately are the surviving copies of Grandma's letters, packed away amongst my personal papers. The letters haven't seen the light of day in years, but just the thought of them brings back warm memories.

I can't wait to find a break in the fast pace of life, pull out a few of those letters, and see what Grandma has to say.

When that happens, it will be a good day.

———

Away I go, in spite of snow

This column appeared on April 20, 2007.

A s I'm writing this I'm trying to wrap up things at work, preparing for a week's vacation.

On the good side, I'm anticipating that vacation. Enough said there. On the down side, I can look out the window down the hall and see yet another day of April snow. That's snow on eight of the last nine days, with more forecast for the coming days. But hey ... ten, 11, 12 ... who's counting?

Around Good Friday I felt like breaking into song: "I'm dreaming of a white Easter."

Part of my vacation preparation is writing an extra column for when I'm away. I would like to believe my readers would be at least disappointed — if not downright crestfallen and depressed — if my smiling face and personal words weren't filing this space today, while I'm away from work.

If you wouldn't have cared whether or not I wrote this column, well, just don't burst my bubble. Please feel free to keep that observation to yourself. But I won't dwell on that now — perhaps it can be a future column. Instead, I'll use this space to vent my frustration with our arctic April.

Actually, I don't mind cool weather. I'll take 55 degrees over 95 anytime. But in April Canada can keep those 20-something degree temperatures, 50-mile-per-hour gusts and single-digit wind chills to herself, thank you.

And I do mind the heavy overcast obscuring the sun for what seems like weeks at a time. My wife tells me I'm solar powered, and I have to agree. I need to see the sun once in a while for the spiritual boost it provides.

I've lived in northwest Ohio all my life, so I'm of course used to the mixed bag of weather that Mother Nature throws our way. I like to follow the weather, compare it to the seasonal norms — and in spring I usually use that as the basis of a sarcastic complaint. Like, maybe ice hockey should be a local spring sport.

Going one step further, I've taken a few famous weather sayings and adapted them to northwest Ohio reality:

March — in like crap, out like crap. (This is the edited version.)

April showers bring May showers.

Nothing is so rare as consecutive sunny days, even in June.

The rain in northwestern Ohio, falls yesterday, today and tomorrow.

Hopefully by the time you read this – more than a week after it was written – the bitter arctic April blast will be a thing of the past. Hopefully Williams Countians are now basking in bright, warm sunshine, the sun's rays raising the spirits of all.

However, if life is dealing us cold lemons in the weather department, we'll just have to make another batch of chilled, cloudy lemonade. We could even raise that lemonade in toast, and sing: I'm dreaming of a white Memorial Day ...

———

cartoons he was the ultimate gentleman, rejecting any idea for "Would You Believe?" that could cause embarrassment or dredge up tragedies of the past.

As enjoyable and important as the cartoons have been, their deepest value to me was as a vehicle in getting to know Russ. It seemed he could find humor in just about anything, anywhere — and often impart a tidbit of wisdom as well.

When I first met Russ and his wife, Virginia, I wasn't yet married. As I grew to know them I was impressed with how much each was a part of the other, and they could often reply to something the other hadn't yet said. Russ and Virginia were quick to offer relationship advice to this soon-to-be married, and later married, young man.

I laughed as Russ and Virginia joked together. I was impressed with their strength and humor as Virginia waged a prolonged battle with cancer. I cried when cancer eventually emerged the victor.

There is much to be gained by having friends from different generations. In his typically observationally humorous ways, Russ gave me a close look at what it is like to grow old. Enjoy life, take hold of it, he advised me many times, explaining that it goes by far too quickly. "One day you wake up and look in the mirror," he said, "and you realize you're an old man."

I drew strength, insight and wisdom from Russ' experience, and the longer I live the more I realize he drew strength, insight, and inspiration from my youth in return.

Ask me how I'm doing, and if the timing's right you might hear, "At least I'm on the right side of the grass." I still appreciate the humor it conveys when I'm experiencing what turns out to be not the best of days.

I hope my own eye conveys a twinkle, my mouth a smile, as I say it.

I've missed Russ since he moved to an assisted care facility near his daughter in West Virginia. I've thought of him often, and cherish the memories of our visits. As time was taking its toll on Russ — as it does with anyone who lives into his 90s — I've appreciated how the perspective of the right side of the grass evolves.

Russ lived a full life, an interesting life as a husband, father, teacher, designer, artist, humorist and historian. Because of Russ, this side of the grass has been a better place.

———

Levies are On My Mind: Time to throw on the old shirt and get to work

This column appeared May 4, 2007.

My column today is like that old T-shirt you wear to change the oil in your car, fix the roof or dig in your garden.

You never really liked the shirt, which is why you first put it on before climbing under the grimy car. You probably didn't buy the shirt yourself, or if you did, later you wondered what you were thinking.

That shirt is old, worn and stained. But you keep it around because every 3,000 miles or so you need it.

Just like this column, which I keep around and pull out of the drawer every primary, general and special election in Ohio.

In Williams County hardly an election goes by without one or more school levies or tax issues on the ballot. This time on May 8 the not-so-fickle finger of financial fate is pointing at the Bryan City Schools and Central Local Schools. Bryan seeks to renew a 5-year, 6.8 mill emergency levy, which raises $1.9 million per year. Central Local asks renewal of a five-year, 6.63 mill emergency levy that raises $615,000 per year.

When each election rolls around I drag out a version of this old, worn but still functional school finance column. Some versions have attempted a detailed explanation of Ohio's system of funding schools — a convoluted mix of a mess if there ever was one, as I've said before. There's inside millage, outside millage, actual millage, effective millage, the 20-mill floor, rollbacks, market value vs. taxable value of property, continuing levies, emergency levies, income taxes ... and more.

I see two key points to the issue — Ohio law won't let income from school districts' voted operations rise with inflation, and the state has been cutting its share of funding for school operations.

So if they hope to keep offering the same programs — or often even to retain a scaled-back curriculum — school boards have to keep going back to the voters with tax issues and levies.

Personally, I believe it's proper to require voter approval to build new schools, or to fund new programs if the money isn't already there. And I believe school boards need to be fiscally responsible and tighten their belts when the local economy is suffering.

But we owe it to ourselves, and to future generations, to be sure our children receive a basic preparation for the life ahead of them.

Perception, as any politician knows, is the key to getting votes. Unfortunately the perception generated by a malfunctioning state system that forces schools back to the ballot again and again is one of greed of financial mismanagement.

In effect, our legislature is allowing schools to serve as a lightning rod for a public frustrated with taxes, high gasoline prices, rising health insurance premiums and a sluggish economy.

I hate to see the kids being burned.

The solution isn't necessarily the old "throwing more money at the schools" cliche. What is really needed is a steady, reliable, understandable state funding system that allows schools to provide the necessary programs without becoming annual cannon fodder for frustrated voters.

Frequent bending of state legislators' ears is the only way to fix the problem. So pick up the phone, write letters, send e-mails. Whichever, just do it.

Quite frankly, I'd love to throw this old work T-shirt away.

Frustrated as you may be, I urge you to go to the polls and support our kids. Vote yes for the schools, both of the school districts.

The kids deserve nothing less.

———

Take time for Mom on this Mother's Day

This column appeared on May 11, 2007.

I n case you haven't caught on, Sunday is Mother's Day.

With all the Hallmark holidays that now fill the calendar, it's tempting to lump Mother's Day in with the others and take the easy way out. Pick up that card and stick it in the mail, call up the florist and arrange that flower delivery.

You know the routine. A few short moments out of your schedule, and you're done.

Sure, the thought represented by the card is nice, and a bouquet of blooms is sure to be appreciated.

I'm guessing what your mother really wants, though, is you — as in your time.

If Mom lives too far away for a visit, pick up the phone. This time, forget about long distance charges and cell phone minutes. Have a true conversation. Ask how she'd doing, and really listen to her answer.

Is there something you can do for her? If she won't come out and say it, chances are if you really listen between the lines, you'll figure it out.

And fill her in on your own life, especially what's good. And even tell her what's not so good — it may do her good to be able to offer a bit of motherly advice. Too, be sure to let her know you appreciate everything she's done for you.

If Mom lives close enough to visit, then do all of that in person. And allow plenty of time for the visit, and savor those intimate moments. As those whose Moms are no longer with us are so very aware, Mom won't be with you forever.

I'm one of the lucky ones in life. I'm ready to hit the half century mark, and Mom is still a part of my life. I can't even begin to express how important Mom has been to me — it goes far beyond the scope of this column. All I can do is repeat that I'm one of the lucky ones, to be blessed with a loving, concerned, caring Mom like mine.

A 10-minute drive will take me to the corner of Stryker's Allison and Defiance streets, the same home where most of my childhood memories reside. I'll get to sit down with Mom and Dad, joined by my wife and sons, my sisters and their families, and enjoy the day. Hopefully we'll be able to convey how important she is in our lives, and make it a day she'll cherish.

Many times our days are so hectic that the chance to visit with Mom, even the chance to pick up the phone and give her a call, is all too elusive. I don't intend to let Mother's Day be one of those days.

Neither should you.

It's easy to forget in this frantic, task-a-minute world we live in, but time really is the most precious commodity we have. You might be able to maximize the enjoyment of the time you have by paying someone else to perform your least pleasant chores, but actual time cannot be had at any price. All the money in the world won't buy you a single second more on this earth than what you're allotted.

So what more precious gift can you give your Mom on Sunday, than some of that time?

———

It had to be one heckofa conversation

This column appeared on May 18, 2007.

The woman obviously was enjoying her cell phone conversation.

She was laughing, throwing her head back at times. She was gesturing wildly, shaking her head, totally engaged in what was being said, oblivious to anything going on around her.

And, frighteningly, she was behind the wheel of an SUV.

Fortunately for her and the vehicles around her, at the time I saw her she was stopped in a left-hand turn lane, just barely inching forward from time to time.

Unfortunately for me, she was blocking my exit from the Main Stop on Union Street.

All I wanted to do was go home for lunch. I was tired from a busy morning, and I was hungry.

And all I could do was just sit there, and sit there, and sit there some more, fuming as my blood pressure began rising by the minute.

I don't know how long she had been in the turn lane before I pulled up to the Main Stop exit. When I first arrived there was a steady flow of traffic in both directions, keeping her from turning. Finally, a car slowed and signaled, turning off a block ahead and clearing a way for the phone-talking SUV driver.

She was of course laughing, gesturing, and totally oblivious.

After the third or fourth gap in the traffic — each time giving the distracted driver far more than enough clearance to complete her turn — the driver of the car waiting behind her honked.

Each successive time the yammering woman in the SUV was given a chance to clear the way, the driver behind her honked again, to no avail. Finally the frustrated woman behind her laid on the horn, still to no avail.

After probably a dozen chances to move had been presented to the obsessive cell phoner, I added my own horn to the ruckus, which now began sounding like a discordant group of braying mules.

By this time my anger had turned to amazement. I could have backed up and pulled around to a different driveway, or turned right instead of crossing the street and driven home a roundabout way. But I was so astounded by the yakking driver's performance, I now had to see it out to the end.

Finally, after what seemed like forever, the woman came to her senses, realized she had a clear path ahead, and pulled into the Main Stop.

All I can say is, I hope it was one heckofa conversation.

Not content to simply go on, I honked to get her attention, which was already again focused on the phone. Getting no response, I laid on the horn, and waved my arm out the window.

When she finally looked, I used my fingers to imitate a phone held to my ear, then made the cut motion below my chin.

She looked at me blankly, then went on.

I doubt I made an impression, but I had to try.

This situation was extremely aggravating, but luckily only mildly dangerous.It's frightening to think what could happen if she was barreling down the highway with the same astonishing disregard.

It is my hope that the cell phone woman — or any other such driver — recognizes herself or himself, and puts the cell phone away when behind the wheel. All I experienced this time was some irritation, and a delayed lunch.

And I was able to eat that lunch at home, not from a hospital bed following a traffic crash.

Or, worse yet, at the meal following a funeral.

———

After all the years and all the miles, she still keeps on truckin'

This column appeared on June 1, 2007

A lthough she's been titled in my name for years, she'll never, ever be mine.

She'll always be Merle's truck.

My father-in-law, Merle Eutsler, purchased the Ford F-150 pickup new in April 1978, before he was even my father-in-law. I still have the original dealer invoice, from Tom Sheridan Ford, now Bryan Ford Lincoln Mercury. The truck is exactly what I would have expected Merle to buy — solid but nothing flashy, and with the heavy duty suspension and 300 cubic inch inline six.

The pickup served Merle well. For years she carried him back and forth between Bryan and Weatherhead in Antwerp. And from the beginning it was his painter's truck, as his business went from part time to full time after his 'retirement' from Weatherhead.

Like her original owner, she's steady, dependable, and always gets the job done.

Mechanically Merle's F-150 is a tribute to what proper care and maintenance will do for a vehicle. Just like clockwork,

Merle had the oil changed every 1,500 miles — that's right, 1,500 miles, not 3,000 or 5,000. And he followed the rest of the maintenance schedule religiously, the chassis lubes, radiator flushes, tire rotations, windshield wiper changes, the whole shebang.

Now 170,000-plus miles later, and 11 years after Merle's death, the truck still needs no additional oil between changes. She still starts after sitting outside on a 10 below zero night, and handles the heat of a 95 degree day. The old, manual three-on-the-tree still shifts smoothly.

Cosmetically, though, the old girl desperately needs a makeover, even though Merle saw to it she had a new paint job years ago. A stylish two-tone green when new, she's now tri-colored — dark green, light green and rust. There's a dent here and there, and the sheen is gone. My wife jokes that it's not a Ford, it's an ORD — rust caused the paint of the F to flake off the tailgate.

Fortunately for the truck's future, the rust problems are with the body panels only. The frame and the suspension are still solid.

The old girl is no longer a daily driver, but she's not fully retired, either. Merle's truck still gets a workout, as a steady helper in our old house restoration project. She carries lumber and drywall, even barn beams and siding.

I enjoy the relative anonymity I get when driving the old pickup. I'm amused at how people react to an older truck — they're leery of pulling out too closely in front of me, but when following they can't seem to get around me quickly enough.

We have no plans to retire Merle's truck anytime soon. A new bumper, body panel patches and rust-free replacement bed lie waiting for an upcoming restoration project — after she's done helping with the house project, of course.

Merle's F-150 will never be a show truck, even after the body work and paint. She's always been a work truck, for Merle, then for my brother in law, my son and now myself. On my watch I don't expect that to change. After all, we're just her caretakers.

She always will be Merle's truck.

———

Summer offers a noteworthy musical event

This column appeared on June 8, 2007.

I t's a real throwback, a great chance to kick back and enjoy the music.

Every Wednesday evening in June and July is concert time, a chance to plop down a lawn chair, sprawl out on a blanket in the grass, or grab a spot on the courthouse steps. And you can't beat the admission price — it's free.

The Bryan City Band is as much as part of summer as baseball, hot dogs, picnics, and fireworks.

On Wednesday notes of "The Washington Post" march drifted across the square during the first concert of the 2007 season, the band's 156th. And it's the 46th year the band has been directed by John Hartman, former music instructor with the Bryan City Schools.

In both cases, it's been an incredible run.

A social event as much as a musical one, the summer concerts offer a chance to chat with friends and neighbors, enjoy a warm summer evening around the square, and tap a foot to the beat. The concerts begin at 8 p.m., but many come early to grab a good seat, and enjoy the lawn party. Kiwanians wind their way through the crowd, hawking pop and popcorn, and dispense refreshments from the club's familiar trailer. Some concert goers finish up pieces of cake or pie, or maybe a dish of ice cream, served up by volunteers raising funds for their church or organization.

Occasionally the sweet smell of barbecue chicken remains in the air, from the suppers offered by other local groups earning money for a good cause.

It's usually old time music — true Americana — that emanates from the bandstand. Brass instruments dominate the bouncing melodies of the marches, and woodwinds lead the way in some of the show tunes. The band's members are local musicians, but occasionally guest performers lend their talents as well.

A number of bandstands at various locations on the courthouse square have been home to the downtown concerts. The latest in that procession is the Connin-Hartman bandstand near the square's southwest corner. This bandstand owes its name to Mr. Hartman and two of his predecessors, John and Dale Connin.

Amazingly, Mr. Hartman is only the fifth director in the band's entire history — its directors have been John Connin from 1852-1884, A.C. Miller from 1884-1888, Professor E.A. Tubbs from 1888-1926, Dale Connin from 1926-61, and Mr. Hartman since 1962.

A bonus for me during the concert season is a weekly visit from Mr. Hartman, bearing the program for the coming performance to be listed in the Times. I look forward to his visits, and I've learned a lot from our conversations.

If you catch that whiff of chicken on the grill some coming Wednesday evening, and see the cars headed downtown, you might want to think about following the caravan.

Just grab a bite, lean back in that lawn chair, and experience the music.

––––––––

In this case, sum of no hits is one big hit

This column appeared on June 15, 2007.

From time to time in the game of life we make a special connection. It all comes together, like the batter's perfect swing that sends the ball sailing into the seats to win the big game, creating a memory that lasts a lifetime.

In my life, Tuesday evening served up one of those big time base hit moments — although actually it involved no hits at all.

The short of it was, Justin Verlander of the Detroit Tigers pitched a no hitter, rare and memorable in its own right. He pitched nine innings against the Milwaukee Brewers and allowed no hits, the first no hitter by a Tigers pitcher in 23 years.

The long of it was, for me the day had been a protracted, wicked one at work. But tired as I was that evening I jumped at Dad's offer to help out with a plumbing project. I was eager for his assistance for a number of reasons — it's more fun to work with help than work alone, I know very little about plumbing, and Dad's mechanical skills far outweigh my own.

Besides, Dad is just darned good company.

Having Dad help with a project actually shaves at least three hours off of every four that I would spend doing it alone. Not only are there four hands instead of two to do the work, but what he figures out before putting something together saves tons of time over me putting it together wrong, then figuring it out, taking it apart and doing it over.

In the background on the radio as we worked that evening was the Tigers-Brewer baseball game. Two good pitchers were facing off, Verlander of the Tigers and Jeff Suppan of the Brewers. It was the third inning before any runs were scored. I heard the yell of the announcer and the roar of the crowd signaling a Detroit homer, but I had my head stuck in the crawl space and had to ask Dad who had hit it.

"Brandon Inge," Dad replied.

Dad and I listened and worked until the sixth inning of the game, when he had to leave to teach a training session. I deduced Verlander had a no-hitter going, but the announcers were mum on the subject, following the old baseball tradition of not mentioning the no hitter so as to avoid jinxing the pitcher.

Too bad Dad had to work, and missed the rest of the game.

Later my wife and I watched the end of the game on TV. We saw an amazing double play by Neifi Perez of the Tigers to end the Brewers' eighth inning. During the commercial break I told Diane I thought the pitcher still had a no hitter going.

The TV announcers, like their radio counterparts, were avoiding the subject. But when the camera zoomed in on an obviously intense Justin Verlander sitting in the dugout, I figured the no hitter was alive. And soon the camera trained on the scoreboard — showing no runs or hits for Milwaukee.

As Verlander struck out the first two batters in the ninth I sat in awe, and I watched the entire team erupt in joy as Tiger right fielder Magglio Ordonez caught a fly ball for the game's final out.

The last time a Tigers pitcher threw a no hitter I had watched the end of that game as well, when Jack Morris pitched a no-hitter against the Chicago White Sox in 1984. There was a difference, though — Morris pitched his game on the road, and Verlander played to an excited, boisterous home crowd.

Sharing the end of Tuesday's game with Diane was special. I wish Dad could have been there as well.

But Dad and l will get together soon enough to discuss that epic game, just as we have for Tigers seasons as long as I can remember. My earliest recollections of Tigers games are with Dad and his little white transistor radio, with Ernie Harwell calling the play-by-play.

Through the years Dad and I have experienced the Tigers winning and losing in the World Series, and attended many regular season games in old Tiger Stadium and current-day Comerica Park.

Verlander's accomplishment will provide some good Father's Day conversation come Sunday. And in the future, when I turn on the kitchen faucet I'll fondly recall that evening with dad, the pipes and the Tigers.

A no hit game, perhaps, but for me another in a series of great hits with Dad.

———

Cranky and discordant, and having loads of fun

This column appeared on June 22, 2007.

A ll right, just ease the crank over a little bit more, push in the button and let down the bucket ... Drat! It slipped off again!

OK, OK, maybe just one more quarter.

You wouldn't think feeding coins into an old-fashioned miniature crane attraction at the Jubilee — just to snag an inexpensive harmonica, no less — could become an obsession. But when your young grandson is beside you, cranking away at another of the cranes, it can really catch on.

This was big stuff to Connor, trying hard to get the claws of the crane bucket to hold on to that harmonica box.

After trading several dollar bills for quarters, and dutifully plopping them into the coin slot, I eventually coaxed the crane into holding on to one of those harmonicas.

That inspired Connor to try even harder, and after a few more of my dollar bills became quarters, he proudly showed off his well-earned harmonica prize as well.

Just what Diane wanted, I'm sure — a husband-grandson harmonica duet.

Connor never did get the crane to hold on to a pair of handcuffs. But he did what his grandpa couldn't — his football sailed through the hole at the Ohio State football toss stand, while mine bounced harmlessly to the ground. And he now has a stuffed Brutus the Buckeye as a trophy of that achievement.

Until Connor came along it had been years since Diane and I had enjoyed the Jubilee — since the kids were young, actually. After the boys outgrew the carnival, Diane and I would walk dutifully around the midway a couple of times each year, grab some Pence's caramel corn and taffy, and then be on our way.

It takes a grandkid to remind you what something like the Jubilee is really all about. If you want to enjoy the world, just experience it through the eyes of a 6-year-old.

For a little while Saturday afternoon I was a kid again, looking back at the time I was a youngster of 6, enjoying the adventure of the Jubilee with my grandpa.

It seems like eons ago, yet in a way it wasn't so long ago at all. The thought drove home to me just how quickly time passes, how fast you go from being a grandson to being a grandpa.

More quickly than I care to imagine, Connor will be too old to enjoy the Jubilee.

But for this year at least I could watch his big smile as he emerged from the Fun House — of course, old enough and tall enough this year to go by himself. And I heard the laughter after Connor encountered his brother Dalton and their cousin, and the three launched water balloons at each other in the water wars attraction.

That 99 cent harmonica I carried home from the Jubilee couldn't have cost me more than $8.75 in quarters — and the one Connor snagged probably cost at least as much.

But there's no way to put a price on that smile as he blew his first harmonica chord — or on that discordant duet we sounded out later in my van, our laughter punctuating the out of tune, out of time notes.

Now, as I look at the harmonica perched on top of my dresser, I hope it's at least another year before Connor is too big to enjoy the Jubilee.

———

Not Bartlett's perhaps, but still quotable

This column appeared on June 29, 2007.

His name isn't likely to show up in a Google search of the world's greatest philosophers, and you won't find him cited in Bartlett's Familiar Quotations.

But I can't say enough about the impact his sayings and thoughts have had on my life.

Bryan's older residents knew him as Gerald "Peg" Allison, one of the numerous Allison brothers of his generation. Folks may well recall meals at his restaurants, the Dining Car and later the Golden Hamburger.

I, however, knew him as Grandpa.

Life for Grandpa meant earning his own way — just about everything he had, he worked for. His dad, my great-grandfather, died when Grandpa was only 10 years old.

As one of the older boys in a large family, he saw his schooling end after the sixth grade and instead he lent his hand to supporting the fatherless household.

Despite his limited education, I remember Grandpa as a very intelligent, perceptive man, a self-taught entrepreneur who loved to find humor in the world. His living room coffee table was never without books and newspapers, and his ever-present magnifying glass for reading.

When I was a youngster, it seemed Grandpa never missed the chance to find out how I was doing in school, what my grades were, what I was studying. He would reward me for good grades, and take me to task for any poor ones — and to him, anything less than an A was not acceptable.

Grandpa stressed how lucky I was to have the chance to attend school. I could see how much he regretted his own limited formal education, but he didn't focus on that. Instead, he worked to see that things would be better for me.

He worked hard to stimulate my mind, but also took plenty of time to have fun, too.

What I realize now, and didn't understand then as I sulked after a poor-grade rebuke, was Grandpa's keen sense of what I was capable of. He expected nothing more — but certainly nothing less, either.

I wish Grandpa could see the effect his efforts have had not just on his grandchildren, but our family's generation to follow.

In Grandpa's world there was no tolerance for whining.
"If the cat was a cow, we wouldn't have to buy milk," was among Grandpa's stock replies to a lame complaint. If you didn't like something, his idea was not to whine, but to do something about it.

Grandpa had any number of pet sayings for addressing life's irritations. I think his "You can choose your friends, but you can't choose your relatives" quote probably strikes home for about anyone coping with family disagreements.

And I suspect a clever saying of my father's, "It's easier to apologize than ask permission," may well be attributable, at least indirectly, to Grandpa as well.

My favorite saying of Grandpa's — I have to paraphrase it here, for a family audience — is very pointed. Why are there more horse's behinds, he would ask, than there are horses?

Besides the smile it brought to me as a young boy, that saying has held considerable value through the years. When someone is being rude, inconsiderate or unreasonable with me, I often think of a horse — and you can guess which way that horse is pointing. Instead of growing angry in these situations, thanks to Grandpa I instead sometimes find myself biting my tongue to keep from laughing.

That saying also helps me keep my own bearings in dealings with others. If I'm going to be perceived as an equine — any member of the equine family, for that matter — I at least try to keep myself heading in the right direction.

———

Inspiration: Like lightning,
or lead sinker

This column appeared July 6, 2007.

How do I decide what to write about?

That's a question I'm often asked regarding my column, and it's not really an easy one to answer.

Ideas can come in the form of an article, a conversation, an experience, even a random thought. Sometimes it's easy — inspiration strikes while I'm at the computer, I have the time available to write, and the words fairly fly from my fingers to the keyboard. Within minutes, a raw concept is a finished product, ready for the page.

Other times the inspirations strikes, but at the wrong time. Sometimes the proverbial light bulb goes off when I'm on deadline, and all I can do is scratch a quick note to myself, or take time to type in a sentence or two of the column.

Ideas often appear just after bedtime, in that hazy transition from consciousness to sleep. Sometimes I'm awake enough to scratch a note to myself, other times I'm too far gone and hope to remember the idea come morning.

I'd love to believe a Pulitzer prize or two have vanished in the never-never land of slumber. But then hey, we all can dream.

When I go back to write a column hours or days after the idea first came to mind, I can't always recapture that initial enthusiasm. An 11 p.m. stroke of genius may be a heavy keyboard clunker the next afternoon.

In the old days the X'ed out typing paper would be pulled from the cast iron Underwood, crumpled into a ball and tossed unceremoniously into the round metal wastebasket — and yes, I am old enough to have pulled the mangled text from my old Underwood, crumpled it up and tossed it into a metal wastebasket.

Today the delete key makes it oh so much easier, if not as satisfying.

Sometimes a column has merit, but doesn't come easily. I know I have something worthwhile to say, I just can't quite say it. So I keep plugging away, and eventually I get it — sometimes after setting it aside for a week or two or three to properly ripen.

At times I have a dozen column ideas racing around my brain, and I can't pin down just one long enough to develop it.

Then there's the opposite end of the spectrum, the occasions when writer's block hits. I can stare at the keyboard, brainstorm, take a walk, or whatever, and it just doesn't matter. The muse has taken a break.

A good example of an easy, it-just-about-wrote-itself column appeared two weeks ago, just after my wife and I had enjoyed the Jubilee with our grandson. The weekend was so much fun, so invigorating, that on Monday I found it difficult to concentrate on my work.

Instead of fighting it, I went with the flow, and channeled that energy into a column.

That column actually grew into two. Watching my grandson's joy at the Jubilee brought back memories of myself at the same age, a young boy having exuberant Jubilee fun with my grandpa.

The thoughts of Grandpa stayed with me as well. Grandpa's been gone for more years than I care to remember — I was only 14 when he died — but his influence is still as much a part of my life as the air I breathe and the ground I walk on. Another week, another column that seemed to almost write itself.

Now this is a new week, time for a new column. And until a few minutes ago, my brain was nearly comatose from writer's block. And anytime I tried to shake past the paralysis and write, I was paged on the phone, called to the counter, or to something needed by personal attention.

Then, like a bolt of lightning from the blue, that oft-asked question came to mind.

How do I decide what to write about?

———

Whether good luck or bad, or no luck at all

This column appeared on Friday, July 13, 2007.

Boy, am I in luck.

For the second week in a row I've been short of time and scraping for a quick column idea, and once again inspiration struck from out of the blue.

It just occurred to me that this column appears on Friday the 13th. It's an instant column topic. I don't even have to add water, just maybe stir it a bit. The toil and trouble leading up to this revelation was just the spice I needed.

I must confess, though, I'm not at all the superstitious sort. I've always thought you can influence your luck through actions, but not charms. And often luck is a matter of perspective. Today's seemingly unlucky break can actually bode very well for the long term, and vice versa.

Who knows, perhaps those seven red lights in a row that stopped you in your tracks delayed you enough to avoid a serious accident. And maybe it was the seemingly fortunate string of green lights that brought another person to the wrong place at the wrong injurious time.

I've written about Friday the 13th before — the black cats, spilled salt, broken mirrors, crossed knives, and shortcuts under ladders. So I won't bore you with that.

What I will share is the history of the day. A perusal of various Web sites reveals several origins for the perception of 13 as an unlucky number.

One site claims the Scandinavians believe 13 is unlucky because the mythological 12 demigods were joined by a 13th, an evil one who brought misfortune upon humans. Other sources claim Christ was crucified on a Friday, and the number of guests at the Last Supper was 13 — the 13th guest being Judas, the traitor.

I don't judge people who are superstitious. If a rabbit's foot makes you feel more comfortable, carry a pocketful of them. If breaking a mirror makes you uncomfortable, then hold on tight to that mirror. And whether you're superstitious or not, it's probably a wise choice to avoid stepping under ladders.

Even though I don't hold much stock in superstitions, I do believe in good and back luck to a point.

As I see it, people generally do make their own luck. The lucky ones tend to be people who've planned and prepared, and put themselves in the right place at the right time while on the lookout for that good break. Others seem to forego planning, twisting in the breeze, and then complain when an ill wind blows.

But no matter how well you plan, how carefully you live your life, you can't control the world. All you really can do is put the odds in your favor — be aware, plan, and pray. After that, you're left to play the hand that's dealt you.

In the final analysis, do the best you can and let the chips fall where they may, be it good luck or bad.

———

He's feisty, flighty and lovable, too

This column appeared on July 20, 2007.

Who, I thought, would ever want a parrot?

Pepper was a feisty, aggressive, loud, messy bird when my in-laws brought him into their home in 1982. When my father-in-law showed me the deep V-shaped cut in his finger — his reward for trying to pet Pepper in the pet store — I couldn't believe they actually still purchased the bird.

With an ear-piercing shriek, Pepper would launch himself from the open door of his cage and fly about their house, scattering seed shells, papers and other loose items in his wake. When I approached his cage after he was closed in for the evening, Pepper lurched at me with his beak wide open, giving the impression he would just as soon rip my nose from my face as look at me.

Several weeks later, during a large family gathering, I found myself watching the red-headed, green-bodied bird. He lurched back and forth as people continually passed by his cage, his half-opened beak serving as a warning.

Suddenly it dawned on me — the poor bird wasn't being aggressive to be mean. He simply was scared out of his wits, and defending himself.

I walked over to his cage, providing a shield from the moving mass of bodies. I began talking to him slowly, softly, soothingly. As he began to understand I wasn't going to hurt him, his ruffled feathers began to relax, and he settled onto his perch. With half closed eyes, he quietly muttered back at me.

Thus began our relationship.

Pepper never did fit in well at my in-laws' home. He wouldn't swear like Diane's dad hoped he would — he's not a talker, he just mutters, laughs, or imitates sounds. My brother-in-law's house was a poor fit as well. Eventually Pepper made a "temporary" stop at our home, while my in-laws went on vacation.

At first Pepper didn't adjust well to us either, throwing a shrieking, wing-flapping fit every time someone approached his cage. But slowly we won him over. He began accepting cheese curls and pieces of oranges — offered at the end of a toothpick, to protect our fingers from the ever-threatening beak.

We ended up feeling an affinity for Pepper, and adopted him into our family.

Eventually, we opened the cage door and allowed him to venture into the living room for exercise. He began to gently accept treats from our bare hands. But it took years for Pepper to trust us enough to sit on a shoulder, and years more to step onto an outstretched hand, and allow his head to be stroked.

Today Pepper still screeches when I approach. Now, though, it's a shriek of greeting, delivered from inside the house as I exit my van in the garage after work. As soon as I step in the door Pepper flies to my shoulder, muttering an excited welcome, stroking my beard with his beak.

Generally, anytime I'm in the house Pepper is on my shoulder or perched nearby. If I fall asleep on the recliner, Pepper nestles up against my chest. When we eat a meal Pepper is there on a shoulder or the back of a chair, sharing our food.

Pepper is intelligent and perceptive. He anticipates our moves and reads our moods. He can be lovable, but neurotic — he absolutely hates certain things, including hard, bright colored candies. If I'm eating jelly beans I need to keep them away from Pepper — otherwise he grabs them from my hand, one by one, and throws them to the floor.

For years Pepper had a housemate, our blonde cocker spaniel Copper. Pepper owned the home first, so he of course trained Copper to his ways. At the supper table Copper not only begged food from the people but from Pepper, too, as the bird perched on the back of my chair. And Pepper would oblige, eating half of a portion and then tossing the rest to the patiently waiting pup.

I'll never forget Pepper's reaction the night Copper died, at the senior doggie age of 14. That night Diane and I stretched Copper's lifeless body on a blanket on the living room carpet, hugging in mourning. Pepper looked on, seemingly frightened almost to death himself, pacing and emitting soulful cries for his lost companion.

For weeks Pepper was visibly depressed — he sat listlessly, barely eating. Slowly, bit by bit, he recovered, returning to his old feisty ways.

Pepper's emotions show in his eyes, in a way I can't really explain. His eyes will dilate with sheer joy, dare I say love, as he cuddles up with us for a relaxing evening. Or they'll narrow in irritation in the presence of a stranger.

Time, though, is advancing for Pepper — like it's advancing for all of us. His energy seems a bit more subdued, those eyes not quite as sharp as in his younger years. Pepper turns 27 this month, elderly for a conure. We've been told by experts his life expectancy is a bit over 30 years, with 35 being about tops.

My entire life I've been fascinated with animals. But through Pepper I've reached a deeper understanding of intelligence different than our own — yet in ways very much the same, with strong emotional needs.

How, I now think, could I ever get along without my parrot?

———

Expect the unexpected;
and stupid things, too

This column appeared on July 27, 2007.

S ome things have to be seen to be believed.

And even if you've seen 'em and believed 'em, some you would just rather not have experienced at all.

Monday morning, about 10:30 a.m., I was waiting at the southeast corner of Main and High, waiting to cross High Street. The light was red in my direction, the "Don't walk" sign plainly blinking in bright red from across the street.

I'm not terribly fond of being a pedestrian at Main and High. I typically wait and watch carefully, and on more than one occasion that caution has been worthwhile. Many times I've had to wait to step out — or even step back out of the way — as a leadfoot driver or inattentive cell phone talker blew through the intersection against the red.

This time, ahead of me as I walked up to the intersection was a young woman pushing a stroller, and two very young children on foot ahead of her.

I stopped in my tracks, dumbfounded, as she proceeded out into the crosswalk against the light with the stroller, the two young children running well out ahead of her. I wanted to say something, but I was afraid of distracting them. A westbound car was approaching on High, fortunately being driven by an attentive woman who slowed down well back from the intersection, allowed the quickstepping, stroller-pushing, red-light-ignoring woman and the two kids to reach the safety of the sidewalk.

The light soon changed, presenting me with the walk sign, and I stepped out into the intersection.

Before the thought was barely through my mind — no, she won't cross again — the young woman again stepped out, with several southbound vehicles now pulling out from just-changed green light at Main and Mulberry. One of the vehicles was a tractor-trailer rig.

I could only shake my head as the two young kids sprinted well ahead of her across the street. Again I wanted to say something, and again I was afraid to distract her. Those kids were only one unexpected car pulling out of a parking space or alley — one inattentive driver — from death or serious injury.

That scene has been running through my mind ever since. Maybe I was wrong in keeping silent, but the safety of those children was utmost in my mind.

It's probably only wishful thinking, but I hope that the young woman reads this column, or hears about it. Regardless, I hope those kids are never again put in that situation.

I suppose there are several common sense lessons reinforced by what I saw. If you are walking with young kids near traffic, keep them close at hand — preferably hand in hand. Obeying the "Don't walk" sign at a busy intersection — kids or no kids — should go without saying.

For drivers the lesson is also pretty clear. Pay constant attention and expect the unexpected.

In fact, expect the stupid. Unfortunately, odds are there is someone out there who won't let you down.

———

Battle of the sexes: Is it trash or is it treasure?

This column appeared August 3, 2007.

Few things can test the strength of a marriage like a garage sale.

Usually the sale itself isn't the toughest part of the test — although 95 degrees and high humidity on sale day can change that pretty quickly. Rather, the worst conflict comes as you're finding things, sorting possessions, deciding what stays and what goes.

If you're married and you've ever had a garage sale, you know what I mean.

"You're not keeping *that*, are you?"

"No no no no no! That was my favorite shirt! I plan on losing that 20 pounds, remember?"

"Yes I'm keeping that old 1979 Ford car radio. I might need it sometime."

It quickly becomes clear — one wife's junk is another husband's treasure, and vice versa.

Some items are no-brainers, like our old bicycles at the last sale a couple of years ago. The bikes had hung in the garage for years, the dust covering was so thick it was hard to discern their colors, and between them they had four flat tires.

And for the most part — favorite shirts aside — clothes are easy to decide on. You know you're not really going to lose that 20 pounds. And thankfully disco hasn't made a return yet.

But other items are truly difficult. No, I don't really have a place for that miniature grandfather clock. Even though it's 50 years old it has very little value as an antique — but it was a gift from Grandpa to Grandma, and I just don't have the heart to part with it.

For at least a year we've been talking about another garage sale, and until now I've managed to dodge the issue. But this weekend is the World's Longest Yard Sale along U.S. 127. And, you may have guessed it, we have a house on U.S. 127.

With the dates now set for us, all that's left is to prepare.

So far we haven't come to verbal blows — heck, we haven't even sniped at each other yet, even though the sale is only two days away as I write this. But there is a reason.

Instead of our usual prolonged, detailed, methodical inventory of property, a prelude to parting with accumulated treasures, we've both been too busy to do more than poke at the surface of our piles. And when we have looked through things, we haven't been together doing it.

We have a few items picked out for sale, like some wonderful old 1800s oak doors with frames that are surplus from our house restoration. We have some knickknacks selected to go. And that antique professional floor model hair dryer will be quite the piece for somebody — but not for us.

But this is definitely going to be a much more casual sale than our norm. The World's Longest Yard Sale runs Thursday through Sunday, but we don't know if our sale will last for the duration.

We will be setting up Thursday, but we won't be fully stocked. We'll still be sorting through things as the sale proceeds, so who knows what we'll come up with, and on what day. And if most of our stuff has sold or the crowds aren't there, we'll close up shop early.

I'll have to say, so far I like this care-to-the-wind approach. In fact, we may try it again if we have a sale next year. The casual approach does wonders to cement the marital bond.

That is, until I happen to find my favorite shirt buried among the clothes at the sale.

———

Life's rule is, if it can go wrong it will, repeatedly

This column appeared August 10, 2007.

Murphy's Law has it right — if something can go wrong, it will.

The irritating aspects of life are indeed inevitable. Since you can't fight the annoyances, and you can't change them, there's no sense in letting them upset you. In fact, my advice is to look for the humor those nuisances hold, and enjoy a laugh instead.

Here are a few of the universal laws of annoyances I've experienced. I'm sure you can add a few of your own.

A thumb or forefinger attracts a hammer better than a nail. And an already bruised thumb or finger attracts a hammer much better than an unbruised one.

When your car tire goes flat it will be in the rain, the snow, or 95 degree humidity.

If you are moving something heavy that can catch on something, it will catch on something.

The number of inches of snow that will fall on a given winter day is directly proportional to the number of miles you are required to travel that day.

The bigger the hurry you're in, the more likely you'll attract a red light. On second thought, it's actually the more likely the light will turn yellow just a second too soon for you to get through.

Gasoline prices will plummet after you've just filled your tank.

Gasoline prices will skyrocket when your tank is nearing empty.

If a groundhog has unlimited acreage in which to live — fields, woods, a stream, wide open rolling ridges — it will instead choose to burrow under your house.

When you drop something heavy and you're not wearing shoes, the object will land on the sore toe that you stubbed the day before.

If you drop a grape on the kitchen floor, it will roll under the refrigerator or the stove — no matter how far away the refrigerator or stove might be.

Should you wish to end a drought, just go camping. Or have contractors scheduled to work outside on your house.

When your wrench slips off a nut, your knuckles will find the hardest, sharpest surface nearby.

If the income tax law is changed, it will come a year too late to give you the greatest benefit.

If the income tax law is changed, it will come a year too early to give you the greatest benefit.

Investment advice to buy low and sell high is much easier in theory than in practice.

When your home water heater gives out, it will be on a holiday.

The deck furniture you've just purchased will go on sale the next day.

Taking a nap is the best way in the world to make the telephone ring.

A batted baseball in the backyard will take the most direct route to a window.

Sage workshop advice "measure twice, cut once," really means measure twice and still end up swearing and cutting again.

It's best to check the bread for mold spots before you've eaten half of your sandwich.

When you are in a hurry and have just one bolt to purchase at the hardware, the person in front of you in line will be having three keys copied.

No matter how deep the drought, weeds will still grow — and the new trees and bushes you've planted and watered faithfully will shrivel and die.

And as any married person can tell you, the answer to your spouse, "Of course I know what I'm doing," will be followed directly by compelling evidence that you don't.

———

Make the time, enjoy it, live life to the hilt

This column appeared August 17, 2007.

W
hen you can, take your time. Enjoy the ride.

You're not going to be on this earth forever.

It's far too easy to focus on your job, on today's list of chores, on what has to get done right now, all while missing the big picture.

Granted, work is important. It's tough to pay the bills without income. I believe in doing a good job, and throw myself into my work — maybe too much. Like many people, I draw a great deal of satisfaction from a job well done and I feel badly if I mess up.

But we all benefit — and in the long run our performance is the better for it — when we can step back a bit, take a deep breath, and put it all into perspective.

I'm not saying to dwell on death or fear our eventual passing. Rather, if we're aware we don't have forever, we're perhaps more likely to accomplish what is truly important.

We'll lose that weight next week, we often say, letting the cholesterol build up in our systems. We'll start exercising in the fall when it's cooler, we say, as our hearts become lazy and flabby, our lungs less efficient.

Some may say they'll go back to school next semester, or look for a job tomorrow, or spend more time with their kids next week.

Well, don't wait. Time is running shorter by the minute.

Last week I was mired in my to-do list, swamped at work, nearly overwhelmed with what needed done at home. I was focusing on anything but the big picture.

When Diane first said she wanted to go to a concert Friday night, I first thought of all the reasons not to go. I'll be too tired, the lawn needs mowed, I haven't picked up the drywall or insulation yet for the house project. Fortunately, something in my inner brain took over. I started to think how much fun it would be to sit back and take in the music, how relaxing it would be to have an evening alone with Diane.

And that in-touch part of my brain remained in gear, conceiving the idea of taking Monday off work to allow a late night Sunday with my sons and grandson, taking in the annual Perseid meteor shower.

Friday afternoon at work did not go well, as I tried to finish up and dash out the door for a few things I had to get accomplished before I could play. But I did get out the door, did get those chores done, and did go to the concert.

The night was even better than I anticipated — enjoyable music and great company. It was back to personal work Saturday and part of the day Sunday, getting insulation and drywall in place, but even that had its moments. And the meteor shower Sunday night was fantastic.

The weather was absolutely gorgeous, with clear skies and perfect temperatures. My grandson spotted a few meteors — one a spectacular flash across the sky — before his eyelids grew too heavy to continue the watch. Stuart, Joe and I got to see a good many more before sleep finally overtook us in the morning's wee hours.

That day off on Monday with sons and grandson was fulfilling as well. Part of the day involved a plumbing repair and work on Joe's '65 Mustang, but the functioning faucet and Mustang ride with the windows down was well worth the effort.

Sure, I paid a price for that extra day when Tuesday morning came. I had to work hard to catch up, and I irritated some co-workers by not being as up to snuff as I should have been.

All I can say to them is I'm sorry, but it was one of those times I had some important living to tend to. When it comes right down to it, I'm sure they understand. Maybe I can pick them up sometime when the tables are turned.

Don't wait for something traumatic, an illness or the death of someone close to us, to drive home how temporary our existence here really is. Instead, seize life while it's good.

Enjoy it. Treasure it. Embrace it. Make the most of it. Take the time to live it to the hilt.

I'm sure my grandson's memories of the meteors and the Mustang will live on long after I'm gone. Who knows, maybe down the road maybe it will inspire him to make new memories with his own grandchildren.

That, to me, is about as big as the picture gets.

———

I love a walk in the woods; my shots are with a camera

This column appeared September 7, 2007.

I love walking alone in a quiet woods on a crisp, cool, sunny fall day. I love the feel of the fresh fallen leaves underfoot, the distinctive outdoors smell, the contrast of the reds, yellows, browns and greens against a clear blue sky.

I love watching a squirrel dart up the side of a tree, a chipmunk dash behind a log, or a deer suddenly appear ahead of me on the trail. I love the gurgling sound of a creek rushing over the stones that create a small rapids.

The stillness, the soft rustle of the wind in the trees, the honk of geese in the distance, all are a wonderful contrast to the usual cacophony of the telephone, the radio, the television, passing vehicles and other sounds of modern living.

My earliest experiences in the woods were with Dad, fishing and camping. They remain some of my favorite memories today. Dad wasn't a hunter, although he's told me his grandfather, my great-grandfather, was an avid one.

I was introduced to hunting as an adolescent, by friends and their fathers. Hunting was a chance to be in the woods, sometimes all day, often in stands of woods I'd never experienced before. Through high school I became a frequent weekend hunter, usually with friends, sometimes alone. Unlike my friends, though, I wasn't upset when I missed a shot at a squirrel or rabbit. I never confessed it, but I even felt relieved when a shot went wide.

I loved the hunt, but I never enjoyed the killing.

When I hunted by myself, I would often just stop and watch a rabbit or squirrel, gun in hand but finger nowhere near the trigger. I enjoyed finding the animal, but I felt no desire to shoot it.

One Saturday afternoon, I was probably 18, I was hunting and saw a squirrel popping from tree to tree. I raised my shotgun and fired.

I missed, I thought, as the squirrel began to scramble further up the tree. But the squirrel slowed, then jumped down from branch to branch to branch, then climbed slowly down the trunk. As I approached the tree the squirrel slowly walked around the tree, then crawled into a small opening between the roots and curled up. I watched it awhile, then touched it and got no response.

On examining the squirrel I found that a single shotgun pellet had penetrated its chest, inflicting the fatal wound.

Watching the animal's slow death bothered me, and has stayed with me to this day.

I never hunted again.

I still love the woods, love camping, love fishing, love hiking. By necessity, not by choice, I did shoot another animal — this summer, a groundhog that kept burrowing into our country basement and wreaking havoc. But I shot it reluctantly, only after it kept avoiding the traps I set, and remembering the week I spent two years ago rebuilding a section of brick and stone foundation the groundhogs had damaged.

I read this week that new figures from the U.S. Fish and Wildlife Service show the numbers of hunters age 16 and older dropped by 10 percent from 1996 to 2006. Even though I no longer hunt myself, I find that trend to be unfortunate.

Although many people neither understand or appreciate it — and on its face it seems contradictory — hunters can play a valuable role in the health of wildlife. With the loss of natural predators such as bears and panthers in many areas, including northwest Ohio, hunters fill their traditional roles.

Nature often isn't kind, but a quick death from a gunshot or arrow seems better than widespread suffering and starvation brought on by overpopulation. Animal populations and hunting harvests are carefully monitored by wildlife officials, and hunting seasons set accordingly.

Too, hunters are guardians of our wild areas. They're willing to back up that commitment with cash, as a major source of funding for wildlife conservation and purchase of land for nature preserves.

If a hunter is acting responsively, shooting an animal as humanely as possible, and is using the harvest for food, not just killing for killing's sake, I respect what he or she is doing. It seems to me anyone who grabs a burger at a fast food joint should really feel the same way.

As for myself, I'll continue my quiet walks in the woods, but I'll leave my gun locked in its case.

If I do any shooting, it will be with a camera.

A car is just a car, a truck just a truck; or is it really?

This column appeared on September 14, 2007.

Wu-rumph.

You know that sound. It comes as you try to start your car on a cold, cold winter morning.

Wuu-rumph. Wuuuu-rumph ... tickatickatickatickaticka.

You need to get to work, you have too much to do, too many places to be. In the chill your spirit sinks as low as the charge in that frozen battery.

For most of us our car, van or truck isn't in the forefront of our mind until it won't start, or the "check engine" light comes on. It's just transportation. At a basic level that's all a car really is — a utilitarian amalgamation of metal, plastic, glass, cloth, vinyl and rubber to get you where you want to go.

Some, however, see their car as far more. It's can be a status symbol — a Lexus, Cadillac, Lincoln or giant V-8 truck. True, it may well be a dream to drive, and give a comfortable ride. But there's more there than just transportation, it's a driver's statement to the world.

To others a car may be a hated or feared machine they are forced to deal with. Or a cash-consuming lemon, sucking in money for repairs that the owner can't really afford, sort of like an ATM in reverse.

Yet others seem to see their vehicle as something to wash and worship, polish and pamper. Always in the garage, oil changed every thousand miles, every speck of dust wiped away, that intoxicating new car smell preserved — and a scratch in the paint is a heartbreaking disaster.

Some of us even see vehicles as a way to hold on to our past, to park a bit of our youth in the garage and resurrect it on a sunny summer day.

As for myself, I need to drive something I can depend on. My vehicle has got to be reliable and comfortable, a machine I can count on no matter how it simmers or freezes. It's got to swim through standing water and surge through the snow.

I'm choosey when I buy a vehicle. I shop and research, then shop and research some more. I need to feel comfortable and confident behind the wheel.

Once I do buy a vehicle, I'm a stickler on maintenance, and typically keep it as long as it's dependable. I don't care if it has a ding or scratch here or there, as long as it works and I feel like I could hop in anytime and drive to Maine or Alabama, or wherever I'm inclined to go.

Right now I drive a van I've had for years. It's anything but flashy, but it's solid and dependable.

I don't look at my vehicle as a status symbol. If someone is judging me by what I'm driving, then odds are that's not a person I care to impress anyway.

But I do appreciate vehicles from the past. My favorite car ever was a '65 Mustang, my college car, and a few years ago I bought a similar Mustang as a toy of sorts. It's simple, I can work on it, it's fun to drive, and a part of my youth is mixed in with that paint and metal.

As if that's not enough, I also have a '78 Ford pickup that's both utilitarian and nostalgic. It's a practical vehicle, carrying lumber, drywall and other odds and ends for our house restoration project. And it holds a special place in our family, as my father-in-law bought the truck new from Tom Sheridan Ford in 1978.

Mechanically the old truck is pretty sound for its age, but cosmetically it needs some help. Originally a very '70s two-tone green, it now has additional highlights of rust.

One thing I can say for the truck, the last bitterly cold winter day when I turned the key, there was no wu-rumph involved.

It was instead a satisfying rar-rar-rar-rar — varoooom!

————

We're not just writers, we're members of the community, too

This column appeared on September 21, 2007.

At a small town newspaper like The Times, a reporter or editor can be the proverbial jack of all trades.

That extends beyond responsibility for a variety of beats or subjects for the paper. It carries over to being active members of the community as well.

We strive to avoid conflicts of interest in regard to positions in local government, of course. But many of us at The Times are involved in clubs, societies, churches, sports and other activities. Many of those organizations provide services or raise funds that help make Williams County a better place to live or work.

Often Times staffers work behind the scenes. We tend to downplay our own involvement in print, instead highlighting the efforts of others.

A good case in point is a local fall tradition, the Barn Fest, and the involvement of Times and Trends Editor Sharon Patten.

She's a charter member of Newlyn Quest, the literary club that initiated and continues to sponsor Barn Fest. Newlyn

Quest was founded in 1967. The club established the Barn Fest in 1977, and for the first seven years Sharon and her husband, Don, hosted the event in the back yard of their former West High Street home.

Sharon said Newlyn Quest member Sandy Bible had seen a similar event, and brought the idea back to the local club. When Sharon was asked if she and Don would be willing to host the event, she said, "We thought it would be a fun thing to do, so we said OK."

The barn behind what was then the Patten's stately home provided the centerpiece for the early events. The initial Barn Fests focused on colonial crafts, and featured an iron kettle of beef vegetable soup simmering over an open fire — a scene still a trademark of the Barn Fest today. She said the first Barn Fest drew 20 exhibitors and 300 people, even though many who attended said they had no idea what a Barn Fest was.

"It was a family event," Sharon recalled. "We had games for the kids. The men stood around the fire and talked, and we had bluegrass music."

No only did Sharon host the Barn Fest, she served as one of the chairs for the event's first seven years.

On a personal note, for those early Barn Fests I had a true bird's eye view — they took place right below my second-floor apartment window. In my bachelor years I had an upstairs apartment in the historic Patten house, an area that formerly would have been a servants' quarters.

On warm Barn Fest days the smell of that simmering soup, wood smoke and heated candle wax sifted in through my open back windows. All I had to do appease my hunger, and check out those colonial crafts, was to walk down my back steps and head out the door.

In 1985 the Barn Fest outgrew the Patten's yard and open field behind, and was moved to the MacDonald-Ruff Ice Arena where it is still held today.

As far as Sharon is concerned, the Barn Fest is still a family event. Her children Heath, Heather and Holly assisted with those early events by selling lemonade and cookies and running errands. Today her daughters, Heather Teegarden and Holly Goodrich, are Newlyn Quest members and are co-chairs in charge of Barn Fest exhibitors.

"They have barn fest in their blood," Sharon says.

This year Newlyn Quest is celebrating the 30th anniversary of Barn Fest. Attendance has grown, from 300 at the initial event to 1,000 in 1985, and typically 2,000-plus to date.

So far Barn Fest has generated $150,000 that Newlyn Quest has in turn invested back in the community. In my opinion, that's what community service is all about.

———

'The War' sparks memories of one vet's service

This column appeared on October 5, 2007.

I found the images and stories of the PBS series The War compelling, even mesmerizing.

In spite of that, my eyes were continually drawn to two small wooden frames on the wall near our television.

One frame, a triangle, holds the now folded flag that covered my father-in-law's coffin during his funeral in 1996. The other displays his patches and decorations from World War II.

Those items tell more about Merle Eutsler's service than he ever shared with his family. The War, for him, was not something to be talked about.

A technical corporal's stripes give away his rank. The tech part came with his job — laying telephone wire to forward artillery units, to allow their fire to be directed by commanders.

The 9-V patch is for his unit, the 95th Division. Merle's division came in on the Normandy beaches soon after D-Day, and fought across Europe into Germany.

As he always did when asked about The War, Merle would deflect any questions about the Bronze Star that now hangs in the frame. He would just change the subject, or make a joke. "Never missed a meal," he quipped when I asked about the medal.

What he never said was the Bronze Star is awarded for heroic or meritorious achievement while in military operations against the enemy, in Merle's case Nazi Germany. Whatever that heroic act may have been, Merle wasn't about to call attention to it.

Among the other awards and service pins in the frame is one medal that stands out from the rest — the Purple Heart.

Only those wounded or killed in combat receive it.

I saw the scars on his abdomen once. "Those are my rooster tracks," he joked, flexing his muscles and effectively thwarting any prying questions.

For years my questions to Merle about The War — just like those from any members of the family — were met by that firm but friendly stone wall. Information simply was not forthcoming.

One evening Merle was visited by one of his World War II comrades, and as they talked they caught up on their lives and shared war memories. For once, Merle opened up about The War, in his private room, over a few beers with his buddy.

I was with them, but made sure not to get in the way.

I kept my ears open and mouth closed for the next several hours as they rehashed their parts in The War. Merle's job laying wire, it turned out, was much more difficult than I ever could have imagined.

He told of getting rousted from his sleeping bag in the middle of freezing, snowy winter nights because somebody cut wires leading to an artillery unit. That "somebody" was likely a German patrol, laying in ambush knowing that an American repair crew was on the way.

Getting pinned down by snipers, unrolling wire through German-held territory, and dodging enemy planes were all part of his job. It seemed the threat of death loomed daily.

Merle described learning about what I later determined was the Malmady Massacre, when German soldiers killed more than 80 American POWs in cold blood. He and his comrade recalled how their own unit stopped taking German prisoners at that point — their officers would no longer accept them.

Merle didn't say what did happen to the prisoners — they just disappeared, he said.

By listening that night I found out how Merle was wounded. He and another soldier were laying wire when a German plane flew overhead. The pilot spotted them, then banked behind a nearby hill.

The soldiers sprinted for a nearby ditch for cover. Merle's comrade made it, but Merle became tangled in his roll of wire, leaving him as an open target when the plane swooped over the hill and opened fire. Pieces of shrapnel struck him in the stomach.

In those days soldiers were patched up and when they healed went back to the front, as did Merle. He continued as part of the American advance into Germany that ended the war in Europe in 1945. His unit was ordered to be a part of the planned invasion of Japan, before the atomic bombs brought the war in the Pacific to an end.

From what he and his friend shared that night, I came to understand why Merle chose to keep that experience in the past.

What Merle did share after the war was a pride in his country, and devotion to fellow veterans. No matter how hot the day of the parade, or how cold or rainy the night of the football game when the flag was to be raised, Merle was part of the color guard.

With Merle's funeral flag in that treasured triangular frame is his Veterans of Foreign Wars hat — the one he wore as a member of the firing squad that honored so many of his fellow veterans, at so many of their funerals.

Including his fellow survivors of The War.

———

Say no again and again, or say yes once?

This column appeared on October 12, 2007.

It's impossible to say no to that parade of shy kids from the neighborhood, each child knocking on the door and tentatively handing you an order blank or block of raffle tickets

"We're raising money for our ..." — and you can fill in the blank, be it the soccer team, the baseball team, the football team, Boy Scouts, or this or that club.

And the call or mailing from a local organization seeking money — be it to fight blindness, or cancer or some other disease, or clothe a child in need for the winter — makes me want to support their worthy causes.

But there's only so much money to go around, however generous our intentions may be. And those repeated telephone calls, repeated knocks on the door, from people with their hands out can be an annoying interruption to our precious free time.

Enter the United Way.

Despite a steady stream of publicity touting the United Way of Williams County, it seems many people really don't understand what the United Way is, and what it does.

In a nutshell, it combines those fund-raising efforts of a myriad of local agencies into one concise annual campaign. No parade of calls and visitors from each and every one of the 32 agencies that receive United Way funding — just one campaign, one solicitation to give.

United Way volunteers also take the guesswork out of that giving.

I don't know anyone who has the time to research each and every agency that asks for a donation, to determine how much of a given donation actually goes toward the group's mission and not to administrative costs or salaries. But collectively, each year United Way volunteers screen all the agencies that are candidates for United Way funding. They approve United Way money only for agencies that demonstrate they are meeting a need in the community, and spend that funding effectively.

Who benefits from your donations to the United Way? Hungry people. Homeless people. People suffering from illness or disability. Kids who can't afford to play a sport. Children who need an adult mentor to help ease the rough spots in growing up. Community members coping with addictions or mental illness. People who find themselves in a temporary tight spot for whatever reason.

Above all, they are local people, right here in our own communities.

This year the United Way of Williams County has a goal of $365,000 for its 2007 campaign, which now is under way. The campaign is asking residents from countywide to contribute, to in turn support programs that help people from throughout the county.

It isn't a Bryan effort, or Montpelier effort, or one centered in Edgerton, Stryker, Edon, West Unity, Pioneer, Blakeslee, Kunkle or Holiday City. It is a countywide endeavor.

This week is the local United Way Week, a special push to showcase United Way's efforts before the public. The Bryan Times is doing its part, running a story each day showcasing a program or process of the local United Way. We do this because, as a newspaper staff, we believe in what United Way is doing to make Williams County a better place.

In my mind the United Way is the way to go — a big, responsible bang for your donated buck.

———

I, while in the kitchen, may well be a biohazard

This column appeared on October 19, 2007.

I f I were a chef, my white hat would be emblazoned with a biohazard label.

I must confess, I can't argue with friends and family's assessment that my culinary skills are somewhat limited.

Stuart and Joe still remind me of the great frozen pizza incident of '84. Diane was in New York state for computer training, leaving the three of us guys to "bach" it for a few days.

In my mind, I deserve some credit. During the entire time Diane was gone and I was in charge of the kitchen nobody suffered food poisoning — at least not to the point of needing medical treatment — and I didn't burn down the house.

That, to me, marked the experience as a resounding success.

The boys, however, remember things differently.

For supper one night I prepared two frozen pizzas. They were too large to place on the same rack in the oven, so I placed one on the top and one on the bottom.

The top pizza, other than some blackening around the outer edges, was fine.

The bottom pizza, I must confess, resembled something uncovered from an ancient site during an archaeological dig.

But in my defense, other than being black, charred, dry and shriveled, it didn't really look all that bad.

Unfortunately that bottom pizza was the one intended for the boys, with their preferred sausage and cheese, and it evoked howls. "You burned our pizza," they protested.

In the telling and retelling through the years the pizza became more charred, more burned, more blackened, and the last rendition I heard depicted it as less appetizing than half-burned charcoal.

What they don't recall is that I was the one who ate the bottom pizza. We switched toppings, and I consumed the crunchy version.

What brings my culinary talents to the forefront this week is a request from Times and Trends Editor Sharon Patten that every Bryan Times staff member submit a recipe for the recipe tab.

Most of our staff members are wonderful cooks and submit great recipes for Sharon's tabs. I am perhaps the lone exception.

For a past recipe tab I shared a recipe for Civil War era hardtack. I don't know if anybody actually tried to make it, but it's one dish I have successfully prepared.

I've thought about a recipe in which you take one cup of corn flakes, pour it in a bowl and then add milk. But with my luck in the kitchen, the milk would probably be sour.

There's just something about cooking that I can't quite grasp. For one thing, it takes too long. It makes no sense to me to cook something for two hours at 200 degrees when an hour at 400 degrees — or even a half hour at 800 degrees — should suffice.

Resident cooks around the Times, however, have failed to grasp the wisdom of that approach.

So I guess I'll fall back on that tried and true recipe, frozen pizzas: Take two pizzas, place one on the top rack of the oven and the other on the bottom rack, and turn the oven up really, really high ....

Or maybe I'll just get Diane to submit a recipe in my place.

————

Half a bubble off plumb is a DIY theme

This column appeared on October 26, 2007.

N othing in the world carries quite the same jolt as an alarm clock on a Monday morning after a week's vacation.

As I write this, my head still is humming from the vibration. It's amazing how easy it is to settle into a routine of sleeping in, and starting off the day in the recliner for a slow read of a newspaper, while sipping that first cup of coffee.

On the other hand, as a newspaper editor I'm amazed at how hard it is to just take in the news — even on vacation — without turning over in my mind how it would play in The Bryan Times.

As vacations seem to do, mine flew by. It was a week of some fun, and some old house restoration. For me, it's a stretch to consider our house restoration as work, because for the most part I find it enjoyable.

But every home project has those not-so-rewarding moments. As our house project has progressed, I have observed some universal laws that every experienced do-it-yourselfer is sure to encounter at some point.

And being unable to take off my writer's hat, even on vacation, I just had to jot them down.

Such as:

If an object being moved can catch on something, it will catch on something.

The lone drill bit missing from the case will be the one you need for the task at hand.

The power tool's plug — or the extension cord you select — will be six inches shorter than the span between the work and the electrical outlet.

The box of screws will contain one less screw than you need to finish the job.

You will realize you are one screw short five minutes after the hardware store closed.

The box of nails will contain one less nail than you need to finish the job (and see above).

Nothing attracts a hammer's blow as well as a finger.

If you can install it backwards, you will install it backwards.

It's measure once, cut twice — regardless of your intentions otherwise.

Every job is five times harder than you think it will be, even in a pessimistic moment.

If the screwdriver in your hand is a Phillips, the screw you want to loosen will have a straight slot.

If the screwdriver in your hand has a straight head, the screw you want to loosen will be a Phillips.

If you have both a straight head and Phillips screwdriver in hand, the screw you want to loosen will be stripped so neither one will work.

The highest concentration of tree roots in your yard lies along the path of the drain line you wish to bury.

No matter how you position your ladder when you paint, the last tiny spot to be painted will be just out of your reach.

If the lightweight, innocuous swing canopy leaning against the side of the house can fall at some improbable angle, and somehow do it with enough force to spill your paint bucket on the deck, it will do so.

The battery powering your drill will run out of juice halfway through drilling the project's final hole.

If there are 376 sizes of something you need to complete your project and the store is out of just one of those sizes, the missing size will be the one you need. And the other hardware stores will be closed. (See above.)

And, no matter how many of these immutable laws I discover, there are more to be found just over the horizon.

———

For a fleeting moment,

I took a step back in time

This column appeared on November 2, 2007

I froze in mid-step when the man emerged from the door.

He had Uncle Rusty's walk, the same gray hair combed the same way, the same lively eyes, the same smile.

My mouth dropped. "Hi, Uncle Rusty," was at the tip of my tongue, before I caught myself.

I took a slow breath, then smiled and nodded at the stranger when he noticed me looking his way.

My Great Uncle Rusty, you see, passed on years ago.

It's amazing how some people leave a void in your life. The years may shroud that void, eventually shrink it. But time to time something happens — a man with a familiar gait and smile appears, or a familiar-sounding voice strikes your ear — and that emptiness is back.

Ironically, I saw Uncle Rusty's lookalike just down the street from the One Stop Shop in Bryan, the building that used to house Bryan's Kroger store. For many longtime Bryan residents Russ Allison's smile was a familiar sight behind a counter or along the aisles of Kroger's, which he managed for many years.

I, too, remember Uncle Rusty in his white Kroger apron. But my favorite memories are from sitting with Grandpa Allison in Uncle Rusty and Aunt Naomi's living room.

I loved hearing the old family stories. The interest they showed in my life, and the advice they would offer, was invaluable in helping me find my way in the world.

Too, I admired Uncle Rusty for the care he showed for his wife, my Aunt Naomi, as rheumatoid arthritis slowly stole her ability to walk, then to sit in a chair, then to sit upright at all. Through it all they never let Naomi's difficulties get in the way of living a good life, of sharing happiness, or making their home a fun place to be.

I find it incredible to believe that Uncle Rusty and Aunt Naomi have been gone for going on 20 years now.

For just a split second, when I saw the friendly looking man, I forgot that Uncle Rusty was gone.

It was wonderful to see him again the other day, even if for a split second in my imagination. I walked away from that encounter smiling, that void he left behind filling with a flood of happy memories.

My Dad was with me when I saw the old man, and I told him how much the stranger resembled Uncle Rusty.

As life sometimes has it, I spoke to Dad again that day. Immediately, from the tone of his voice on the phone, I knew something was wrong.

"Your Uncle Don died," Dad said, getting right to the point. My uncle had died that afternoon, not too long after Dad and I had finished our weekly lunch together.

That night, I drifted off to sleep with memories of Uncle Rusty and Uncle Don Zwayer circling in my mind. Through the years my contact with Uncle Don has been sporadic — he and Aunt Pat and my cousins lived in Tulsa, Okla., where they had moved when I was quite young. But I spent time several summers visiting there, and Uncle Don always warmly opened his home to me.

Uncle Don succumbed Tuesday after a long illness, and we knew his passing was only a matter of time. Even so, he leaves behind a void in many lives — in the case of Aunt Pat and my cousins, I'm sure it's a very large void indeed.

Fortunately for his friends and family he left memories that, as time passes, will continue to generate smiles.

———

Woodhenge can be memorial to half a century

This column appeared on November 9, 2007.

Perhaps we'll call it Woodhenge.

I figure the garage frame of hand-hewn timbers can serve as my 50th birthday memorial.

There are different ways to celebrate — or as some do it, mourn — life's milestone birthdays. I celebrated one of mine Saturday, complete with black balloons, black crepe paper, black over-the-hill greetings and even a black rose.

I took the approach, however, that my mood was not going to match that dark tone. The way I see it, half a century of survival is cause for celebration, not sorrow.

Some folks prefer quietly ignoring such a birthday. Others go for lavish parties. I think either way is fine, depending on your outlook and taste.

I opted for practicality, with a dose of fun mixed in.

My wife asked how I would like to spend my birthday. With weather fit for outdoor work winding down as winter nears, I figured my 50th — since it fell on a Saturday — was a perfect day to put up the frame for our garage. To match our historic old farmhouse, we've salvaged some ancient hand-hewn timbers to create a garage that will look like an outbuilding that's been there forever.

Once it got too dark to work, we decided, the bonfire party would start.

Even the fire had a practical purpose, as we wanted to burn the pile of wood and branches left over from cutting down a hollow tree beside the garage site.

I've never been much for large parties, so I elected to keep it a low-key family affair. Nothing fancy, just vegetable soup simmered over the fire, hot dogs for roasting in the flames, the usual finger foods and snacks, and cider, coffee and hot chocolate.

Nature was kind, offering a bright, clear, cool, starry night, ideal for gathering around the warmth of the fire.

We even were treated to a surprise fireworks show.

As luck would have it, some neighbors apparently also had something to celebrate. They set off a miniature version of a grand fireworks finale every hour or so throughout the evening, drawing our oohs, ahs, and applause.

I'll have to say I felt pretty special that night, celebrating with the people I love the most.

We cut the garage work short on Saturday, halfway from completion, to get ready for our family guests. So Sunday afternoon my work party continued, with sons, a sister, a brother-in-law and a friend pitching in.

In short order the timbers were in place, and I have to say I was a bit awed. I had never taken on a project like that before, and had no idea how it would go.

Had I tried it myself the garage never would have gotten off the ground, pun fully intended. But with help — especially the design and plans by Dad, making use of his engineering background — the garage thus far has turned out better than I ever could have imagined.

As we admired our handiwork, we joked how much the frame resembled Stonehenge. I decided to christen it Woodhenge, at least until the roof and siding are complete. Who knows, maybe the new "old" garage will witness future family 50th birthday parties — a son, or a grandchild perhaps — another few decades down the road.

———

Locally, this is no man's land for The Game

This column appeared on November 16, 2007.

Wherever your allegiance may lie, Williams County is sure a fun place to be as the Ohio State-Michigan football matchup approaches.

You could call Williams County no man's land, ground zero, the front lines as the verbal battles for one-upsmanship rage. It's the modern day version of the Ohio-Michigan War, perhaps the greatest sports rivalry in the land, and the county's allegiance between the schools is deeply divided.

So many local folks have ties to Ohio State — they attended OSU themselves, family members or friends earned their diplomas there, or they simply share the state's allegiance.

But with the northern edge of Williams County bordering on Wolverine country, the same can be said about the many local fans who support Michigan.

Reverberations of past OSU-Michigan matchups still resonate in my ears. I grew up in a home that bled scarlet and gray during the college football season. Maize and blue were banned colors in my home come fall.

Ironically, I came into the world the year the Buckeyes won their third national collegiate football title, in 1957.

I may not remember that great OSU season, but many illustrious Buckeye seasons do remain as vivid memories. Who could ever forget the 1968 national champion OSU team that crushed Michigan 50-14, and defeated O.J. Simpson and the USC Trojans in the Rose Bowl?

On the day of The Game — being OSU vs. Michigan, enough said — the family gathered raucously in the front TV room. We cheered the great plays, mourned over the poor ones, jeered the referees.

After all these years the clouds of dust kicked up by Woody Hayes' conservative OSU offenses still blow around in the breezes outside the Allison homestead in Stryker.

I'll have to admit I'm not the rabid Buckeye fan I once was. My college path took me to the University of Toledo, where the Rockets have accumulated football legends of their own.

Replacing my disdain of the maize and blue of Michigan is a solid allegiance with the gold and blue of Toledo. Even though it's a down year for the Rockets, I still wear those colors proudly.

But a soft spot remains in my heart for the Buckeyes. In fact, I sat in that familiar front room of my boyhood home Saturday for part of last Saturday's OSU loss to Illinois, which knocked the Buckeyes off the pedestal of the nation's top ranking. It was a sad day for the old Allison homestead.

But at this point there's little time to mourn. After all, come this Saturday, the Buckeyes will invade the big house in Ann Arbor.

And come Saturday the TV at the Allison house in Stryker will be tuned to The Game. I'm not sure if I'll be watching The Game there, but I can guarantee there will be a contingent of Allisons in that front room carrying on the tradition, cheering, groaning, yelling and jeering.

And hopefully, when it's all said and done, they'll be celebrating, too.

———

Rockwell might be missing, but it's still our own charming scene

This column appeared on November 23, 2007.

I smiled at the visitor's reaction. "This is so neat," I overheard her say.

That out-of-town young lady, a friend of a friend of my son, said she'd never seen anything quite like Santa's arrival in Bryan. She seemed awed by the occasion — the music of the marching band, the crowd of kids greeting Santa, the season's first lighting of the downtown square.

Actually, her reaction reminded me of a child's wonderment on Christmas morning.

I drove home that evening with an appreciation that has stayed with me since.

Growing up in Williams County, it was a simple fact of life that the Friday after Thanksgiving was when Santa came to Bryan. It seemed as set in stone as Thanksgiving or Christmas Day itself.

As a very young child I remember freezing my toes as I stood in line with Mom, gazing up at the courthouse lights, waiting probably not-so-patiently for my turn on Santa's lap. I still remember how tremendously long that line of kids ahead of me seemed, how big Santa appeared to be and how good the Spangler candy cane he gave me tasted. Later came my cynical teens and early 20s, when I would avoid anything as campy as Santa's arrival parade.

But soon came another turn in the cycle of life, and again my toes were freezing, again the line seemed to stretch forever, again I was waiting not-so-patiently. Santa seemed smaller this time, though, as I held my young son's hand while he eagerly anticipated his turn on Santa's lap.

Of course life's cycles continue, and now the excited pair of eyes on the square that special Friday night belong to a grandson. Watching him exchange a high five from Santa, experiencing the reindeer on the square, and staring up at the bright lights on the courthouse is still a highlight of my life.

You don't have to be from out of town to appreciate what we have right here in Williams County. If it's not too late, grab your coat, grab the kids if you've got 'em, and head on down to the square.

Santa Claus is coming to town.

If you don't have time to catch tonight's 6:30 p.m. parade — or if you just plain enjoy St. Nick — you can catch him in a parade at Montpelier at 6 p.m. Saturday, the culmination of a daylong celebration in the village. And Santa will be putting in appearances around the county as the season progresses.

I plan to be on Bryan's square tonight. Life's cycles still are turning, and this time our family group will include a grandson now old enough to be skeptical of Santa's existence.

Norman Rockwell might not have painted the scene, but it's the very definition of small town Americana.

And it's right here in our own back yard.

———

I'm a fan — er, fanatic — with an annual case of indigestion

This column appeared on November 30, 2007.

The term sports fanatic should never have been shortened to fan.

Regardless of the sport, regardless of the season, there are fanatics whose emotional roller coasters follow the tracks of their team's wins and losses, successes and failures.

For example, on Thanksgiving Day the indigestion many folks suffer has nothing to do with the holiday feast. It just happens to be they're Detroit Lions fanatics.

Ask me. I know. I'm a Lions fan, and the Lions play every Thanksgiving. This year my own Thanksgiving Day digestive discomfort was fueled by Brett Favre and the Green Bay Packers.

It's interesting to me to consider how and why people become fans of certain teams — even how those favorite teams follow along generations.

For example, I'm a diehard Detroit Lions fan. I have no illusions why — I follow squarely in the footsteps of Dad. Growing up I spent fall Sundays in front of the TV with

Dad, expressing our shared frustration with the latest Lions failures.

I still remember Dad's outbursts against Detroit quarterback Milt Plum, his grumblings that they should have kept Tobin Rote or Bobby Layne. I'll never forget the 5-0 Lions playoff loss to the Dallas Cowboys in 1970, and learning that then-Detroit quarterback Greg Landry was so nervous he was throwing up on the sidelines. It's sad to think Landry was the Lions last Pro Bowl quarterback.

And come Thanksgiving Day, Mom was kind enough to plan our feast perfectly — for halftime of the Lions game.

Some folks come by their fanatic status in other ways. My oldest son, for instance, is a Pittsburgh Steelers fan. I'm sure it resulted from the Steelers' dominance during his younger years.

And I'm sure he learned watching Detroit games with me that the Lions were not likely to be worth getting passionate about.

We have fun sharing football with our separate favorite teams. We'll watch each other's teams, and offer our mutual support. Usually we watch the playoffs together — and nearly every year there are Steelers games. But Lions playoff games are a decidedly rarer commodity. Lions playoffs wins are even rarer — in fact, blue moons seem common by comparison.

I must say the Lions haven't always been also-rans. Even though sportscasters seem fond of saying the Lions are among the teams that have never won a Super Bowl, that's quite misleading. The Super Bowl is simply the current name of the game to decide the NFL championship, and the Lions have won multiple NFL championship games.

They actually won one of those championships in my lifetime, a 59-14 shellacking of the Cleveland Browns. So what if it was 1957, and I was only a month old.

A championship's a championship, right?

I must note the Lions frequently are mentioned when records are discussed. For instance, Monday night's game between the Steelers and Miami Dolphins was played in abysmal rainy conditions, and the Steelers won 3-0 on a field goal with only 17 seconds left in the game.

It was noted that the last time a game was 0-0 that late into the contest, the Detroit Lions were involved — a 1943 scoreless tie with the Giants.

And for the Dolphins the Monday night loss took their season record to 0-11. The last time a team started the season with more consecutive losses was in 2001. The team? The Lions, of course, who started 0-12 that year.

For Lions fanatics, you see, the turkeys don't come just on Thanksgiving.

———

Marketplace may change, but memories will remain

This column appeared on December 7, 2007.

I was walking among nearly empty, depressing shelves. My mind, however, was back in a more pleasant time.

Miller's New Market in Bryan had not yet opened to the public when I first set foot inside. I was part of a group from The Bryan Times invited to preview the grocery just before it opened in January 1991.

We were greeted by a bright, crisp, modern store and friendly staff members, and we sampled items from the store's deli.

That's the Miller's I choose to remember.

I was driving home after work on Nov. 28 when I decided to make one last visit to Miller's. The store was preparing for its closing, a victim of a changing market. I knew most items were marked down to half price and decided to make that final stop.

Apparently, many others had been there before me. I was shocked to see the bare shelves and how few items remained. I found some premium sardines, canned clams and bags of sunflower seeds, and that was about it.

As I checked out I learned the store was closing for good that evening, a bit ahead of the original schedule. The decision, the cashier said, had just been made.

A mix of sadness and end-of-the-shift tiredness showed in the eyes of the remaining workers. It had to be tough on many of them, I know, losing their jobs just as the holiday season was beginning.

Miller's for me was a store of convenience. We live on the east side of town, and it was a quick trip there for us to replenish our pantry. We felt loyalty for the store, too, as our youngest son had worked at Millers part-time as a high school student.

I remember the Bryan Miller's manager, Larry Robinson, from my high school days when he was with Tiny's Pizza on the square. He has always been friendly, always had a smile, anytime I have encountered him through the years.

Never in my life have I tasted commercial beef jerky as good as the store brand sold at Miller's. I'll miss having the jerky so readily available, and now I'll have to remember to stop by the Montpelier Miller's when I'm in town there.

Through the years Miller's has been open on the mornings of many holidays, including Thanksgiving and Christmas, and it's been a saving grace when we've needed a last-minute missing ingredient.

It's surprising what memories a store's closing can prompt. I know I'll forever be grateful for Miller's when I recall our Christmas morning of 1999.

We had arrived home on Christmas Eve after attending funerals for my uncle and grandmother in Alabama. Mom and Dad arrived home even later that night. They had departed home quickly, with shopping for Christmas dinner probably the last thing on their minds. Now I knew Mom was upset that she had no idea what to feed the family on Christmas Day.

Miller's came to the rescue. On our way to Stryker Christmas morning Diane and I stopped by Miller's — as far as we knew, the only grocery open for miles around that day — and picked up a giant platter filled with ham, chicken, vegetables other goodies.

Thanks to the Miller's workers who gave up part of their Christmas morning, a difficult day for our family was just a bit easier to bear.

When I drive by the empty Miller's building I'll try to push aside the depressing image of the last day's empty shelves. Instead I'll recall the bright, full aisles to which I became accustomed.

And I'll wish to best of luck to the Miller's workers, the Miller's management members who made a heart-wrenching decision to close the Bryan facility, and the success of the other stores in the Miller's system as they work to adapt to our changing times.

———

A bunch of old toys to some, a reminder of heritage to me

This column appeared on December 14, 2007.

To most folks walking by, it was a collection of old toys.

Sure, it caught people's attention that the toys were like new, bright and shiny in their original boxes, and were made at the former Strydel-Emenee plant in Stryker. And some parents and grandparents recognized a toy or two they had played with as kids — even though most of them weren't there to look at the toys, but had bundled up their youngsters for Santa's arrival in Stryker.

When I saw the display the toys became almost transparent. What I saw instead was Mom, who had four young children to care for when she made the decision to enter the workforce 40 years ago, accepting a job at Strydel-Emenee. I was the oldest, still in elementary school, and felt important when just a bit of responsibility for my younger sisters fell on my young shoulders.

I remember Mom shuffling her work at Strydel-Emenee among the various shifts when she could, allowing her to be home at the most opportune time for taking care of her family. Whenever needed, Dad would pick up the slack. Those shifts changed through the years, as Mom adapted to the various needs of her growing kids. No matter the shift she was working, I remember she always made sure I enjoyed home-cooked meals, clean clothes, and a house that was picked up, swept and vacuumed nearly daily.

As a child I had no clue just how difficult it is when both parents hold down a full-time job, and still put their all into raising their family. Now, having had my turn as a parent, I understand.

Those old toys a atop the tables at the Stryker brought it all home to me, in a way I had never fully appreciated before. It was a great idea for the Stryker Area Heritage Council to display a sampling of the Strydel-Emenee products, kindly loaned by the firm's parent company, the Ohio Art Co.

For more than 40 years, from 1962 until its closing in 2004, Strydel-Emenee plant produced all sorts of toys.

I thought Mom would enjoy viewing some of the toys she helped create through the years, so we invited her and Dad to accompany us. I had no idea just how much Mom would appreciate that chance — or what a great experience it was for me to be with her there.

As I listened to Mom describe how the toys were made, and what her job was in molding and assembling many of them, I recalled noticing how tired and sore she was after some of those long shifts. I also remember that it never seemed to slow her down.

She'd still share the highlights of her day with us — while she was cooking the upcoming meal, or while we ate it. She'd tell about the Emenee organ line, unconsciously massaging her hand that had placed so many of the screws that secure the organ's top.

As we continued on down the display at the depot Mom talked about stringing the guitars, performing different assembly jobs, and pointed out parts she was responsible for placing.

Most likely, Mom had hot stamped the chrome on the red plastic floor model jukebox that was part of the display. Anytime that jukebox was being produced, she said, she was assigned to do the chrome stamping.

Mom was obviously proud of her role, and she should be — not just for the toys she helped create, but for what her work meant for our family. We never worried about lacking for anything we really needed. When this or that was required for school, or when the time came for college, Mom and Dad's backing was never a question at all.

Actually, their backing has never been an issue, no matter what the situation.

Thanks to that display of old toys, I received a welcomed, unforgettable reminder of that.

———

A Christmas spirit jump start was just what I needed

This column appeared on December 21,2007.

This year, my Christmas spirit needed a jump start.

On Tuesday, I found my booster cables.

As empty nesters, Diane and I have been long removed from school Christmas programs. We were reintroduced this week. Our grandson is a first grader at Montpelier, and we watched him perform in his school's Christmas program for first- and second-graders.

I found a whole new perspective as a grandparent. I watched the young parents — many juggling impatient preschoolers — as they strained to see the parade of pupils and proudly waved and pointed as their child went by.

I could sense the excitement of the kids as they took their places on the risers, savor the joy in their voices as they sang the Christmas carols.

Finally, it felt like Christmas.

Until this week I've found December to be fairly draining. I don't really mind the cold and snow, but what I don't tolerate well is December's nearly constant darkness and lack of sun. It saps my energy. The festive lights of

Christmas decorations help make my spirits a bit brighter, but they can only go so far.

Of course, this energy shortage comes just in time for the mad holiday rush. With parties, errands and shopping, we seem to cram an entire month of activity into the first two or three weeks of December, to get in all in before Christmas.

And the crass commercialism of the season seems more oppressive to me each year. The barrage of Christmas music starts now before Halloween, a two-month assault on your senses whether you like it or not.

The ironic thing is, there's a lot of Christmas music I enjoy. Some of my favorite Christmas memories from childhood involve sitting around the record player or the radio, enjoying the holiday carols. I love listening to a Christmas CD of our choice as we trim the tree, or wrap presents. But for me that enjoyment comes well into December, with a chill in the air and Christmas approaching — not on a warm October day, when most of the leaves have yet to fall.

Now, finally, my spirit has caught up to me, and the time has come to enjoy the Christmas season. The tree has been up and decorated for a couple of weeks now, our holiday shopping is nearly done, and the parties and programs are past.

Now I'm looking forward to a quiet family weekend. I can't wait until Diane and I — perhaps joined by our sons or grandson — set up our traditional assembly line for baking and decorating our Christmas cookies.

Christmas always has been about family, gathering together, enjoying meals, exchanging gifts. The people may change — now I spend time with a grandkid instead of grandparents, and nieces and nephews instead of aunts and uncles — but that special bond remains.

Few things in life are more magical than singing "Silent Night" while our family circles the darkened church with the rest of the congregation, bearing candles as the Christmas Eve service comes to a close.

A kids' Christmas program jump started those holiday feelings for me. If you need a boost, I hope a friend's call or letter, a neighbor's smile, a stranger's friendly gesture, kids singing a Christmas carol — whatever it takes — is coming your way.

May you and yours enjoy a Merry Christmas, and a happy New Year.

———

It's time for reflection, I'll take a look in the mirror

This column appeared on December 28, 2007.

The coming of a new year typically lends itself to reflection, some new years more so than others.

This is one of those "more so" years for me.

I celebrated a milestone this year, my 50th birthday. I stress the term celebrated, because that's indeed how I choose to view it. I spent that birthday surrounded by family and friends, creating a priceless memory.

Celebration aside, however, I do find the half-century mark to be a wakeup call.

I've survived 50 years, and I'm thankful. It's very sobering to realize not all my boyhood friends and acquaintances have been so fortunate.

Just last week, the 20-year-old-daughter of a friend died after a lengthy battle with cancer. My thoughts keep turning her family, to how difficult it must be to cope with the loss of a young daughter, sister, granddaughter, a niece.

I was deeply touched by the stories of Chelsey's courage and faith that her family members shared with me, and how comforting that faith truly is to the loved ones still here on earth.

The death of a young person — especially a bright, vibrant young woman like Chelsey — drives home the fact that life can be unfair and unpredictable.

We're only on this earth for a limited time, and we don't know how long that time will be. It's easy to forget that fact and take life for granted.

I believe it's important to be aware of our own mortality. We don't need to dwell on it in a morbid or depressing way, mind you, but to use that awareness to motivate us and keep us on track.

We only get one crack at this life, so we need to make the best of it. How we live that life has more impact on those around us than we often realize — hopefully, for the good.

As I reflect on this new year, I count myself a very lucky man. Those closest to me definitely have impacted me for the good. I'm very fortunate to have my mom and dad still with us, as important, integral parts of my life. I can only hope if they rely on me in years to come, I can be there for them like they have for me.

I am lucky in many other ways as well. I'm blessed with a great wife, my soulmate. Both our boys are living in the area, and we have a wonderful grandson in our lives. My sisters, too, are all nearby. I can watch my nieces and nephews grow into mature young men and women.

I've even been blessed with a special pet, a parrot that came into our lives by chance more than 25 years ago. He is older now, slower in flight, in the twilight of his life, but he shows me affection each day in a way that transcends the difference in our species.

My list can go on and on — a rewarding career, an instilled and insatiable quest for knowledge, a wonderful historic home to restore, great friends, and so much more.

The years of my wonderful life's past may be growing and the years of my future dwindling, but I'll let that serve as my reminder to make the most of what I have left. I want to leave something worthwhile behind, to follow in the footsteps of the many who enriched my life while they were here.

As a good friend used to reply when asked how he was doing, I can say that for now at least I'm on the right side of the grass.

And for me it's very green, green grass indeed.

———